The Bird Feeder Book

The Bird Feeder Book

*How to
Build Unique
Bird Feeders
from the
Purely Practical
to the Simply
Outrageous*

Thom Boswell

A Sterling/Lark Book
Sterling Publishing Co., Inc.   New York

Design: Chris Colando, Thom Boswell
Production: Elaine Thompson, Chris Colando
Photography: Evan Bracken
Illustrations: Charlie Covington
Mechanical Drawings: Doug Stoll

Library of Congress Cataloging-in-Publication Data
Boswell, Thom.
    The bird feeder book : how to build unique bird feeders from the purely
practical to the simply outrageous / Thom Boswell.
      p.   cm.
    "A Sterling/Lark Book."
    Includes index.
    ISBN 0-8069-0295-7
    1. Bird feeders--Design and construction.   2. Birdhouses--Design
and construction.   I. Title
QL676.5.866 1993
598'.07'234—dc20

                                         92–40584
                                         CIP

10 9 8 7 6 5 4 3

A Sterling/Lark Book

Created and Produced by Altamont Press, Inc.
   50 College Street
   Asheville, NC 28801, USA

Published in 1993 by Sterling Publishing Co., Inc.
   387 Park Avenue South
   New York, NY 10016, USA

© 1993 Altamont Press

Distributed in Canada by Sterling Publishing
   c/o Canadian Manda Group, P.O. Box 920
   Station U, Toronto, Ontario, Canada M8Z 5P9

Distributed in the United Kingdom by Cassell PLC
   Villiers House, 41/47 Strand, London
   WC2N 5JE, England

Distributed in Australia by Capricorn Link Ltd.,
   P.O. Box 665, Lane Cove NSW 2066

Every effort has been made to ensure that all the information in this book is
accurate. However, due to differing conditions, tools and individual skills,
the publisher cannot be responsible for any injuries, losses, or other damages
which may result from the use of the information in this book.

Printed and bound in Hong Kong

ISBN 0-8069-0295-7

Contents

Introduction

If you've never built a bird feeder or house, a wonderful adventure awaits you. Not only are they fun to build and a great way to ornament your yard, you'll get to watch them being used by a fascinating variety of birds you may barely have known existed. If you've already tried your hand at this craft or installed storebought structures, this book will inspire you to stretch the limits of your imagination and skills, and will even help you design your own.

There's something in this book for everyone, from children to experienced woodworkers. While most of the projects are constructed of wood, you'll be introduced to several other accessible materials and techniques as well. And while each project is explained with specific instructions, you are encouraged to adapt and experiment with these designs to suit yourself. Essentially, this book contains the "blueprints" for forty fascinating bird structures, yet it also serves as a manual that will equip you to exercise your own creativity.

Providing shelter, food and water for birds is a human pastime that extends far back into history. In medieval Europe, this was actually a way of harvesting birds to supplement their own meager diets. Native Americans used to hang gourd houses for purple martins who would chase vultures away from their meat drying racks. Gardeners like to attract certain birds to help control insect populations that can destroy vegetation. Martins, robins, wrens, thrushes, warblers, swallows and bats are all excellent exterminators and reduce the need for chemical pesticides.

Of course, there are other reasons for nurturing our feathered friends that are less self-serving. As human civilization continues to encroach on

wilderness, we are obliged to provide habitat for species that have been denied their natural feeding and nesting sites. We can also lure species back into refurbished areas they'd been forced to abandon.

Birding, or bird watching, is growing in popularity, especially in the U.S. and the British Isles. People have a natural appreciation and concern for birds. Sitings are compiled in "life lists," and copious field notes document behavior. The best bird structure designs are those which utilize this sort of information.

Constructing habitat for birds need not be such an exacting science, however. Many a bird will find comfort in even the most amateur of attempts at feeder or house building. Neither may it matter to you precisely which species comes to feed or takes up residence in your generically constructed house. The antics of sparrows can be just as much fun to watch as the flitting colors of a finch.

There are others yet who see these structures as an art form. A "house" need not be a "home," and a feeder or bath can be elaborately sculpted for the absolute delight of humans, yet be nothing more than a curious perch for birds. People who dabble with doll houses or miniatures will love the possibilities of art for the birds. In fact, some of the more detailed and exquisite structures in this book would be better appreciated indoors than out.

As you can see in our gallery (pages 30–49), most examples of this art form are houses instead of feeders. Curiously, feeders are more popular than houses. Maybe it's time to start elevating feeders to the level of art, too, as this book begins to do. Whether for function or fancy, you can take part in this enjoyable creative process.

"Eats Diner" by Randy Sewell

Design Considerations

Types of Feeders

There are several basic types of feeders, each designed to dispense certain feeds and to accommodate the feeding habits of different birds. These are some of the features to consider when choosing a design for your feeder:

1. Maximize the load capacity of the feed container for less frequent refilling.

2. Make the feed container easy to open to facilitate refilling.

3. If there's a roof, it should effectively protect the seed from rain and snow.

4. Provide drainage outlets in the feed tray to prevent stagnant pooling of water.

5. Incorporate a spill tray with a lip or plexiglass wall so birds can see the feed.

6. Provide adequate space for birds to perch and eat.

7. Make it as easy as possible to take apart and clean.

Here are the most common types of feeders, each of which has many design possibilities:

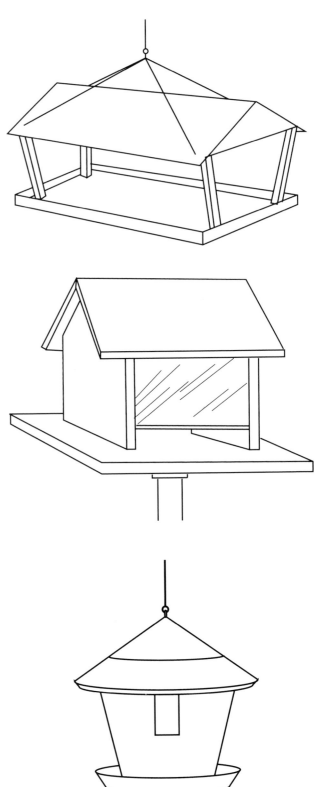

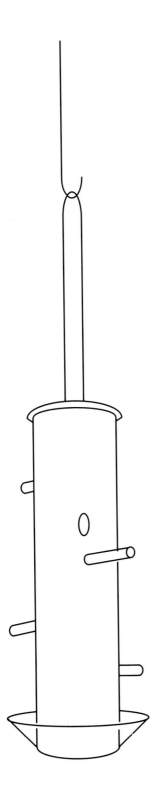

Ground or Open Tray feeders are among the simplest of approaches to dispensing feed. You can attract a wide variety of birds, such as cardinals, jays, sparrows, doves and chickadees, by scattering cracked corn or mixed seed directly on the ground. Choose a clearing of cropped lawn, dirt or patio and sprinkle seed over an eight-foot circle. However, constructing a simple post-mounted tray has several advantages for you and the birds. If you add a lip to contain the seed, allow for drainage with gaps in the lip or holes in the tray. This type of feeder should be mounted about five feet above ground and is very easy to refill and clean.

Roofed Tray feeders protect feed from the elements. The roof should be larger than the tray, and can be supported by a center post, peripheral posts, or even suspended from above. This open-air structure lends itself to all sorts of pavilion and gazebo-type designs, and is a highly functional feeder.

Hopper feeders are quite prevalent because they incorporate so many desirable features. The major feature, in addition to tray and roof, is a feed container that gradually dispenses feed through some sort of openings, usually onto the tray. The roof may cover both hopper and feeding tray, or the hopper only. Some of the walls might be transparent.

Tube feeders are very popular, usually clear plastic to display the feed, and mounted on post or by hanging. They have multiple holes with perches around the cylinder for feeding stations, and often feature a bottom dish and protective roof dome. They are easily refilled, and may incorporate metal-reinforced holes and perches that squirrels cannot chew.

Suet feeders require different structures because of the globular consistency of the suet. A plastic-coated wire cage works well. One-inch diameter holes can be drilled in a hanging log, post or stump and filled with suet. An inverted hanging cup (coconut half, yogurt canister or bell) packed with suet will attract chickadees. These can be hung from a tree or the eaves of a house, or fastened to a tree trunk. They are especially visited in winter, and attract woodpeckers, nuthatches and mocking-birds, among others.

Mesh Bag feeders are very simple and can also be attached to other sorts of feeders. Just fill a plastic mesh bag (such as onions are sold in) with nuts or thistle seed, and hang it to attract finches, buntings and chickadees.

Many birds prefer to light on a good vantage point and survey the situation before swooping down to feed or bathe. If there are no trees or tall structures in the vicinity of your feeder or bath, you can build a simple perch or two. Nail a short cross-piece on top of an 8'–12' pole and plant it nearby.

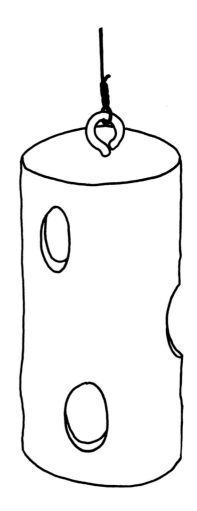

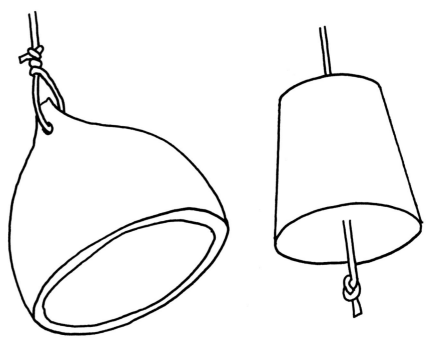

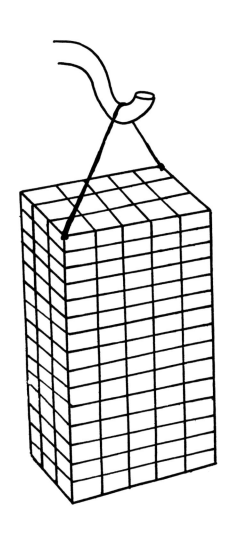

Types of Baths

All birds need water for drinking and bathing. Most birds scoop water into their bills and tilt their heads back to drink. Others, like doves, can actually sip. Bathing behavior includes some fascinating variations as well. Many birds stand in shallow water and funnel it into and out of their feathers using complex body movements. Some take a quick dive and fly out while others fully submerge for a bit. Birds will also bathe in rain or dew drops.

Your bath will be visited more frequently if you place it near a feeder. It can be on or above the ground. When making or purchasing a bath, keep in mind that it should be shallow with gradual slopes so that birds can wade in to a depth of no more than three inches of water. The surface should not be slippery. Avoid ceramics if the water will freeze in winter because they will crack. Concrete works well and can be molded, especially when reinforced, into any shape on or above ground. You may want to incorporate one or more small pools in your landscaping. Even an inverted trash can lid will serve the purpose.

The sound of running water is especially attractive to birds. This can be achieved in several ways. Drip hoses and mist fountains are commercially available for this purpose. You can also erect a reservoir, such as a bucket, over your bath that has a tiny drip hole. This will, of course, require refilling.

Birds also need water during cold dry spells in winter. To keep the water in your bath from freezing, you can purchase an inexpensive electric water heater that is designed for bird baths. Scrub out your bath periodically with fresh water and a brush.

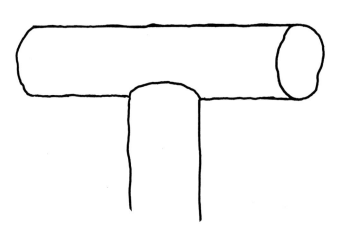

Types of Houses

When you consider how many birds take up residence in unlikely nooks and crannies, it would seem that they're not very particular about housing requirements. However, each species has its own specific needs regarding the dimensions of its living chamber, the size and position of entry hole, siting, etc. Also, it is surprisingly difficult to lure most bird species into man-made houses. Even the colors you paint your house will affect its habitability. Birds generally prefer natural muted hues, although purple martins are attracted to white.

The chart on the following pages lists guidelines for many common species, but bear in mind that birdhouse design is not an exact science. You can learn a lot simply by observing the behavior and nesting habits of whatever birds are common in your region. Build the chamber or platform according to the size of the bird you wish to attract. Place it in a site comparable to its preferred habitat. If it builds nests in the open, it should prefer a platform type of house. If it nests in a tree hole or other crevice, you will need to construct a chamber. Note which species are common to your area and alter your designs to accommodate them.

It must also be noted, however, that a number of designs are intended more for human amusement and decoration than bird utilization. Bird structures have become an art form in their own right, and are displayed in parlors and galleries as well as backyards and public parks. And who knows, maybe some odd bird will share your aesthetic and adapt its needs to your sense of whimsy.

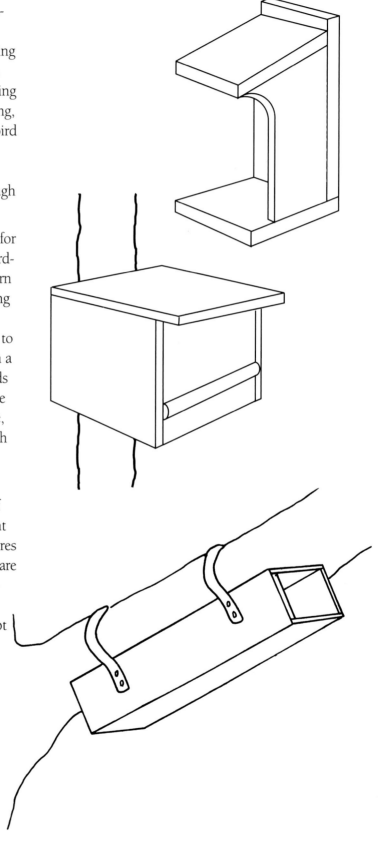

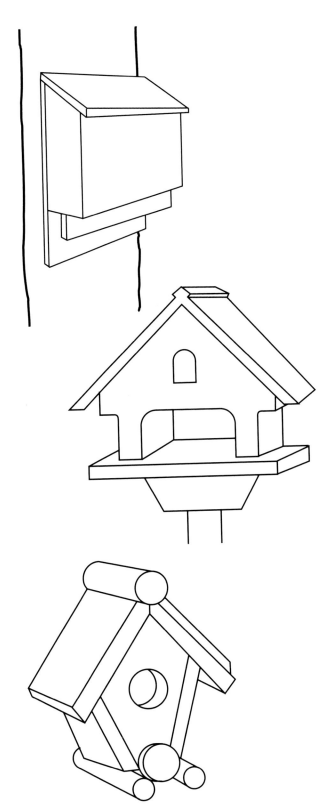

Most bird houses can be divided roughly into four categories, each of which offers numerous design possibilities:

Platform houses are preferred by certain claustrophobic species such as robins. They can be mounted on a pole, cradled in a tree or hung on a wall. They occasionally have one or two walls which facilitate wall mounting or act as a windbreak.

Open Box houses can vary significantly, depending on size, siting, and which part is left open. Barn owls can do without a roof when the box is inside a much larger structure. Kestrels and flycatchers like having one wall open. Bats need open floors for bottom entry. Mounting and siting will vary greatly depending on the species.

Enclosed houses are the most common since they appeal to the widest variety of birds. The floors of these chambers are recessed in the sense that the entry hole is above floor level. There is tremendous variance in all other design elements, mounting and siting.

Multi-Compartment houses have very limited appeal, being suited only to communal dwellers like purple martins and bats. Purple martin houses are mounted high on poles or rooftops. Bat houses are mounted high in trees or on poles. The number of compartments can vary greatly.

Some House-Nesting Birds

Species	Approximate Dimensions	Hole Dimensions
Bluebird (Eastern, Western, and Mountain)[1] Sialia spp.	Floor: 5" x 5" Interior height: 8" to 10"	Height above floor (centered): 6" (5" for Warbler) Diameter: 1-1/2"
Chickadee (Black-capped, Boreal, and Carolina)[2] Parus spp.	Floor: 4" x 4" Interior height: 8" to 10"	Height above floor (centered): 6" Diameter: 1-1/4"
Finch (House and Purple) Carpodacus spp.	Floor: 6" x 6" Interior height: 6"	Height above floor (centered): 3"–4" Diameter: 2"
Flicker Colaptes auratus	Floor: 7" x 7" Interior height: 16"+	Height above floor (centered): 12"+ Diameter: 2-3/4"
Flycatcher (Many varieties) Tyrannus spp., Myiarchus spp.	Floor: 6" x 6" Interior height: 14"	Height above floor (centered): 6"+ Diameter: 2"
Jackdaw (Corvus moredula)	Floor: 8" x 8" Interior height: 12"	Height above floor (centered): 6" Diameter: 6"
Owl (Barn) Tyto alba	Floor: 10" x 18" Interior height: 18"	Height above floor (centered): 4" Diameter: 6"
Owl (Saw-whet, Screech and Little) Aegolius acadicus, Otus asio and Athene noctua	Floor: 10" x 10" Interior height: 15"	Height above floor (centered): 10"+ Diameter: 3"
Pigeon (Street) Columba livia	Floor: 8" x 8" Interior height: 8"	Height above floor (centered): 4" Diameter: 4"
Purple Martin (Progne subus)	Floor: 6" x 6" Interior height: 6" (each compartment)	Height above floor (centered): 1-3/4" Diameter: 2-1/2"
Robin (American and English)[3] Tardus migratorius and Erithacus rubecula	Floor: 6" x 6" Interior height: 8" (open roofed platform)	No hole, open-sided roofed box
Sparrows (House and many others) Passer domesticus, members of Family Fringillidae	Floor: 10" x 10" Interior height: 15"+	Height above floor (centered): 6" Diameter: 1-1/2"
Wood Duck [4] Aix sponsa	Floor: 6" x 6" Interior height: 14"+	Height above floor (centered): 12"–16" (9"–12" for Kestrel) Diameter: 3" x 4" (oval) Add interior ramp covered with chicken wire
Woodpecker (Hairy, Red-bellied, Red-cockaded, Red-headed, and Yellow-bellied Sapsucker) Picoides villosus, Melanerpes carolinus, Picoides borealis, Melanerpes erythrocephalus, and Sphyrapicus varius	Floor: 8" x 8" Interior height: 24"	Height above floor (centered): 9"–12" Diameter: 1-1/2" (Hairy, Red-bellied, Red-cockaded, Sapsucker) 2" (Red-headed)
Woodpecker (Pileated) Dryocopus pileatus	Floor: 4" x 4" Interior height: 14"	Height above floor (centered): 10" Diameter: 4"
Wrens (House, Bewick's, Carolina, and others) Family Troglodytidae	Floor: 4" x 4" Interior height: 8"	Height above floor (centered): 4" Diameter: 1-1/4" (House), 1-1/2" (Bewick's, Carolina, and others)

[1] House will also serve: Tree Swallow (Iridoprocne bicolor), Warblers (Parula spp.), Spotted Flycatcher (Muscicapa striata)

[2] House will also serve: Brown Creeper (Certhia familiaris), Downy Woodpecker (Picoides pubescens), Nuthatches (Sitta spp.), Tufted Titmouse (Parus bicolor)

Height Above Ground	Siting Tips
5'–10'	On fence posts, stumps, utility poles, tree trunks, etc. Place around open fields or any grassy expanse (park, cemetary, golf course). Predator collar suggested.
6'–15'	Locate near large trees, Line with non-aromatic wood shavings.
8'–12'	Both birds primarily Western though sometimes found in East. Purple Finch prefers wooded site.
6'–20'	Site on tree trunk, line bottom with 3"+ of non-aromatic sawdust.
8'–20'	Prefers wooded site, natural-appearing house.
10'+	Away from human noise.
12'–20'	Locate near open fields/meadows to provide hunting range.
10'–30'	Near water if at all possible. Prefers open yard with few or no trees nearby.
10'+	Prefers a perch.
Above reach of cats	Prefers open area near well-maintained lawns for feeding.
12'	Habitats vary widely.
10'–20'	Locate on trees or buildings.
12'–20'	Wood Duck: Locate near (or above) water, line with 3"+ non-aromatic sawdust, predator collar suggested. Kestrel: Site on edge of field or meadow to provide hunting range.
12'–20'	Site on tree trunk, much prefers natural-looking house (bark lined, for example)
6'–10'	Locate among large trees. Natural-looking house essential.
6'–10'	Site on edge of woods, in fencerows, etc.

[3] House (nesting platform) will also serve: Barn Swallow (Riparia riparia), Phoebes, Eastern and Say's (Sayornis spp.), Various Thrushes (Cartharus spp.), Song Sparrow (Melospiza melodia), Pied Wagtail (Motacilla alba)

[4] House will also serve: American Kestrel (Falco sparvarius), European Kestrel (Falco tinnunculus)

Your birdhouse will be occupied only a few months each year by migrating birds. Wait until spring to clean out the house to allow winter birds like chickadees and bluebirds to use the old nesting material. To enable cleaning, design one panel of your house to be hinged or removable. It could be the roof, floor, or any wall. After you have removed all the old nesting material, pour boiling water over the interior to kill any remaining parasites.

Most houses will benefit from ventilation and drainage. Small holes or slots can be cut around the roof eaves for vents. Drill 1/8" drain holes in the corners of the floor.

The entry hole is a crucial part of any house. If it's too large it will invite intruders. If it's too small or high it will hinder access. If it's too low it will admit harsh weather. To discourage predators, you can cut a doughnut-shaped piece of 1 x stock that conforms to your entry hole and attach it inside to extend the portal. Roughen this tunnel with a rasp to accommodate the grip of bird claws.

Varying the shape and material of the roof is a great way to add interest to your birdhouse or feeder. Some basic shapes to consider are shed, gabled, hip, mansard, gambrel, pyramidal, conical and domed. Materials can include solid wood, plywood, bark-faced slab, cedar shakes or doll house shingles, tar paper, fiberglass shingles, sheet metal, copper, bamboo and thatch. Generally, the steeper the roof, the less it is prone to leaking. Just make sure the ridge is caulked to seal it. A flat roof requires the protection of an impervious sealant, as do the edges of plywood where the glue seams of lamination will separate.

Unwanted Guests

It's a jungle out there—and that's just the way it should be. As much as we might prefer well-mannered songbirds with exquisitely colorful plumage, nature's panorama reminds us that the weak must fall prey to the strong, and there is beauty in all creation. Swallows and swifts may clog our chimneys with their nests, but they also devour tons of bothersome mosquitos.

Ultimately, human intervention plays its part in this grand scheme. We are free to nurture and protect our feathered friends with food and shelter. And to do this effectively, we must learn how to counteract the competition and predation that would undo our efforts. Here, then, are profiles of the bird world's ten most unwanted list.

Sparrows

Most varieties of sparrow will nest almost anywhere, including your attic if they find entry. If you've built your house for a less common species, you'll want to discourage them from setting up housekeeping. Since they tend to nest earlier in the season than most birds, you can probably clean out their nests before your intended guests arrive. Also, they are much less likely to nest if you leave off the porch under your entry hole.

Sparrows will also be frequent customers at your feeder. This is really not a problem, unless your feed is limited or you're hoping to attract different birds. If you don't want sparrows, stock your feeder with red proso millet, Niger thistle and peanuts.

Starlings

There's no easy way to keep starlings from nesting in your birdhouse. Like the sparrow, the undesirability of the starling has mostly to do with its commonality. Your best bet is to build your birdhouse strictly to the specifications outlined in the chart on pages 14 and 15.

There's little competition at most feeders, however, since starlings are primarily suet-eaters. Keep this in mind when you stock suet for other birds.

Cats

Be aware of feline territories when you install a birdhouse or feeder. Let's face it, cats love birds, but assuming they're domesticated they will play-fully torture a bird rather than consuming an honest meal. Mount your house, bath or feeder above leaping range. Install a predator barrier on tree or pole. Put a bell on your cat's collar. Eliminate low foliage where cats can hide as they wait to pounce, and keep grass mowed around feeders.

Dogs

Dogs aren't nearly as dangerous as cats, but can still pose a threat if you don't take precautions. You could perhaps verbally discourage your dog, or your neighbor's dog, but you'll most likely have success by fencing the bird zone away from dog territories. A dog's very presence can keep more timid birds from visiting your beautifully prepared sites.

Raccoons, Skunks and Oppossum

If you live in a rural or semi-rural environment, these predators may be looking for a quick meal. Follow the same precautions necessitated by cats, plus a tight mesh fence. You may also elect to control the threat by setting out traps. We would encourage the use of live traps, such as the Hav-a-hart brand. If you believe you must kill these animals, check with your local fish and game authorities and know what you're doing.

Hawks and Shrikes

An attack by these large birds on smaller birds would be natural and horribly fascinating, but

quite unlikely. If you'd like to create a defense for your smaller birds, provide them with lots of near-by places to seek shelter should they be assaulted. The most likely marauders are the sharp-shinned hawks in the eastern U.S. and Cooper's hawks in the western U.S. Do keep in mind that hawks are protected by laws, as well as nature's plan.

Squirrels

These cute little creatures are probably a bird's most prevalent pest. The squirrels' legendary attraction to bird feeders can become a consuming preoccupation for us as human hosts, but needs to be taken in perspective. You may as well expect a certain level of squirrel piracy as inevitable.

Since your goal is to keep squireels away from the birds' feed, let us look at a number of methods. Hang or post mount the feeder at least twenty feet from the nearest tree and six or more feet above the ground. The post should be slick metal. You can incorporate conical or disk-shaped baffles at least four feet up the post or on any wires used to hang the feeder. Any other barriers you incorporate into your design should be made of metal or tough plastic to prevent squirrels from chewing through them.

As a last, or even preventive resort, you can offer cracked corn or whole cobs of dried corn to dis-tract squirrels away from the more expensive seeds intended for song birds mounted higher up. The corn can be dispensed on the ground or up in trees. Cobs of dried corn can even be spiked onto propellor-like squirrel feeders mounted on trees that keep squirrels occuped while providing humans with goofy entertainment. You may even find that squirrels are just as much fun to watch as most birds.

Predator Barriers

Birds will be much more able to experience the peaceful enjoyment of your feeder, house or bath if you install physical barriers to prevent the inevitable harassment of unwanted guests. These barriers are particularly effective against four-legged intruders.

Poles, posts and trees can be fitted with a sleeve of aluminum sheeting that will defy the traction of claws. It must be installed at least five feet above ground level. If you have a metal pole, it wouldn't hurt to grease it.

Conical foils can be constructed out of aluminum sheeting to fit both round and square posts. Join and attach the assembly with self-tapping sheet metal screws, which can be installed with an electric drill. Position the foil at least four feet above ground level.

If your bird structure is suspended, use heavy wire instead of rope. Squirrels can climb down and gnaw through rope. You can also install metal pie pans as baffles on the wire to foil dauntless intruders. The wire can be attached to another wire spanning two trees or man-made structures, but a feeder should be at least twenty feet from a tree or other tall structure to be out of jumping range.

Yet another way to impede cats is to spread chicken wire just above the ground beneath a feeder or house. This will compromise their ability to leap because they will be unable to build up speed on the ground.

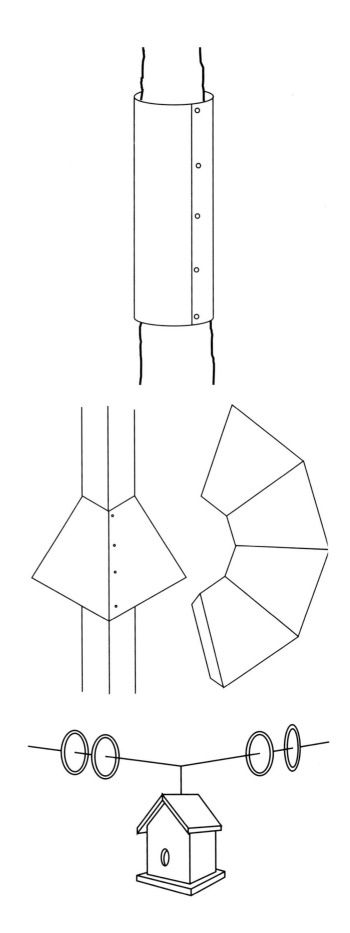

Mounting

Most birds will probably prefer houses that are firmly mounted on a post, tree or wall. Yet this does not rule out hanging, especially for feeders. Observe all siting specifications before planning how you will mount your structure.

If you hang something from a tree, wrap the branch with fabric or inner tube rubber where you attach the wire to prevent damage to the tree. Make sure the branch is strong enough to support the structure.

When mounting a house or feeder to the trunk of a tree, it is preferable to use a batten. This is a vertical plank, almost twice as high as the structure, which reduces the stress from the protruding center of gravity. Use galvanized screws, or a strong strap around the trunk, to attach the batten to the tree. Use galvanized hardware also when attaching a structure to a wall.

Posts can be metal or wooden. Use pressure treated lumber or cedar, whether square or round. Sink the post at least 18" using a post hole digger. Add gravel at the bottom for wood. Concrete isn't necessary, but pack the dirt well around the shaft. The top of a metal pipe can be threaded to fit a floor flange attached to the base of your bird structure. Wooden posts can be reinforced with metal L-brackets or wooden triangular braces at the top.

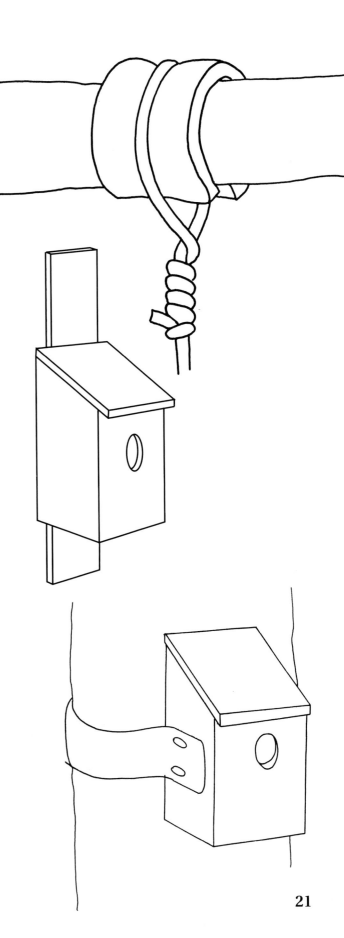

Siting

There are several things to consider when choosing an appropriate site for your feeder, house or bath. You will want to create an environment that is especially attractive to birds. Providing food, water and shelter is a good beginning. Placing these near trees, shrubs and flowers is another way to enhance a bird habitat. You should emphasize any of these elements which might usually be missing in the surrounding area. For instance, on the plains, introduce trees. In the desert, provide water. During winter, display food.

Birds prefer border habitat like where an open meadow or lawn meets the edge of a grove of trees. This allows unobstructed access and egress while maintaining proximity to food, nesting materials and safe haven in the forest.

Feeders can be moved gradually closer to your house as birds get accustomed to using them. This will give you better views of the birds from your window. In fact, some feeders are designed for placement directly at your window for optimum viewing.

Orient the entry hole of a house away from prevailing wind-driven rain. To attract the more timid birds, houses and feeders should face away from the activity of people, such as sidewalks, driveways and children's play areas. Avoid sites that receive extreme sunshine. For the more open nesting boxes and platforms, a sheltered and reasonably hidden site is preferable. Refer to the chart on pages 14 and 15 for more specific site requirements.

If your yard lacks the appropriate vegetation, consider some creative landscaping to attract birds to your habitat. For instance, pyracantha has beautiful berries that birds love in winter months. Sunflowers are another sure bet. See what you can grow in your area.

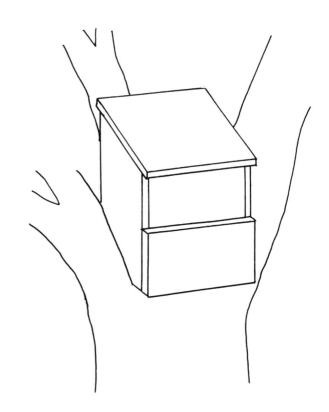

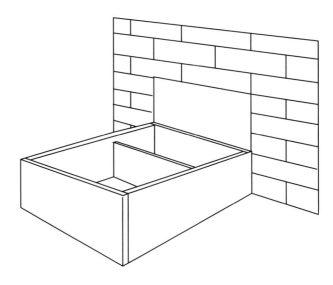

Construction Basics

Materials

There are no ideal materials for building bird feeders and houses. Moisture will eventually take its toll in the form of rot and rust, even undermining glue joints and finishes. Other factors such as sunshine, temperature fluctuation, toxic chemical components, expense and availability must also figure in to your choice of materials. Let's examine the most likely options.

Solid Wood is still a favorite choice, being both aesthetic and easy to work with. One disadvantage, however, is that it's commercially available only in 3/4" and greater thicknesses. If you have access to a thickness planer, this can be remedied. Otherwise you may encounter limitations having to incorporate such thick boards in your miniaturized designs. Another shortcoming of conventional lumber is the knots and other flaws that can complicate the assembly of small structures. It's worth the small extra expense to purchase the higher grades of lumber.

Many of the designs in this book call for pine, but you should feel free to substitute more rot-resistant or elegant species wherever you choose. These include cedar, redwood, cypress, and various tropical woods like banak. Locally you may find yew, black locust, fruitwoods and others. Western cedar is widely available and inexpensive, but its aroma may keep some birds such as chickadees from nesting in houses made of it. Clear-heart redwood is great to work with, but it costs at least twice as much as cedar. If you want to mix woods, be aware that stock thicknesses between species usually vary slightly, which can complicate accurate joinery.

Even though pressure-treated wood is rot-resistant, it should be avoided, except as mounting posts. The chromated copper arsenate with which it is treated doesn't belong with bird feed or tiny nestlings.

Plywood offers several practical advantages. It is strong, unlikely to warp, inexpensive and available in many dimensions. Of the many types, only marine- or exterior-grade plywood and oriented strand board are recommended for bird structures. The others either lack weather resistance or contain toxic substances. Still, with any plywood, care must be taken to seal any exposed end grain against weather.

Marine plywood is superior in that it has no voids, even in the inner laminations. Exterior plywoods are graded by letters which indicate the quality of both faces. For bird structures, use A-C or B-C, and face the better surface outward. Oriented strand board, not to be confused with particle or flake board, is all the same grade. Each of these plywoods is available in standard thicknesses of 1/4", 3/8", 1/2" and 3/4".

Plastics offer some unique possibilities. Tube feeders utilize PVC or clear plastic cylinders. Plexiglass is preferable to glass when used as windows in hopper feeders. Plastic sheeting can be curved and bent with heat, cut with fine-tooth blades, and joined with glues and bolts to form durable structures.

Adhesives usually need to be reinforced with nails or screws. Yellow carpenter's glue lacks water resistance but holds adequately when under roof and reinforced with metal fasteners. Two-part epoxy is expensive but sometimes necessary to bind critical junctures where no other fasteners can be used. Clear silicone caulk is quite effective in both sealing and adhering. A hot-melt glue gun is a handy tool for making waterproof seals, though the glue has relatively low adhesive strength.

Fasteners should always be corrosion-resistant. Nails and screws should be galvanized steel, stainless steel, or brass. Hinges, latches or other hardware that is exposed should never be plated. Use solid stainless, aluminum or brass.

Finishes are actually used on wood more for structural and aesthetic reasons than to protect it from weathering. Unsealed wood expands and contracts as it exchanges moisture with the atmosphere, thus stressing the joints. Heat affects this process unevenly since only certain areas are exposed to sunlight, causing more stress. Even so, structural considerations need not overrule your appreciation for the beauty of naturally weathered wood. The small seams of bird structures will usually withstand these stresses.

Stains will help seal the wood while enhancing its look. A clear top finish can also be added, but must be compatible with the stain. Alkyd stains are oil based. Acrylic stains are water based, easier to apply and clean up, and longer lasting. Clear coatings include polyurethane, marine spar varnish, and penetrating oils which need to be reapplied every year or so. Exterior-rated primers and paints work well, but avoid those which contain mercury.

Any finish you apply must cover all surfaces of the wood, once all glue seams are dry. Pay close attention to all exposed end grain, especially on plywood. Let the structure dry thoroughly at least two weeks or until no odor lingers before letting birds use it.

Concerning the dimensions given in the materials lists, 1 x 12 is a stock size for dressed lumber which actually measures 3/4" x 11-1/4", whereas 1" x 12" means just that. Watch for the inch (") marks. Also, the exact dimensions of a finished component may not always be listed, but the stock needed to make the part is listed.

Tools and Techniques

The projects in this book cover a rather wide range of difficulty. A child can make some, while others require an experienced woodworker. Most, however, are very manageable for anyone with moderate craft skills. In fact, building small-scale projects such as these is a wonderful and inexpensive way to develop your talents. You may soon become inspired to design your own.

Many of the projects require only simple hand tools: hammer, screw drivers, saws and a crank drill. Other tools will be required for specific projects: whittling knife, side cutters, pliers, files or chisels. A power drill and a coping saw will come in handy. All sorts of power tools will improve efficiency and accuracy if you have them, but are not absolutely necessary: jigsaw, hole saw, band saw, planers, routers, etc. However, a table saw is more or less required for about half the projects.

Most of the joinery used throughout these bird structures involves butt joints. Although they are the weakest of all joints, they are quite adequate for small structures, especially when properly glued, nailed and reinforced by other intersecting boards. Miter joints involve two beveled edges butting together, such as roof peaks, wall corners and molding that trims corners. Gluing is crucial since fasteners will not hold as well as with butt joints. However, miter joints seal all the end grain and present a neater appearance. Dado joints include several variations

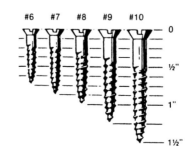
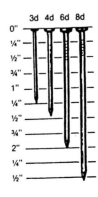

and are rarely used here. They generally require a table saw and are quite strong when accurately fit. Dado grooves are used for movable panels as well as the sort of multiple partitions found in martin houses.

To create a strong glue joint, there should be a minimum of gaps between the adjoining pieces. Cuts should be made smoothly and evenly, and the pieces should be held together tightly until the glue has dried. Good gluing technique is especially important for plywood, since fasteners won't hold well in the laminated grain. Always use plenty of glue for maximum seam strength. Excess can be wiped away after clamping, unless you plan to use stain, a clear finish or to leave wood unfinished. In that case, use just enough glue spread inside the joint without squirting and dripping outside the seams. Trim away any excess *after* glue has dried using a knife and sandpaper.

Screws hold better than nails but are compromised when penetrating end grain, and nearly useless in plywood endgrain. Unless the wood is very soft or the screws are very slender, holes should be pre-drilled to a diameter slightly smaller than the screws being inserted. You might also consider using corrosion-resistant threaded nails, but only for permanent joints since they cannot be removed.

To cut small entry holes in solid wood, a power drill with a spade bit can be used. A hole saw works nicely for larger holes and for plywood. A coping saw can be used if you lack a hole saw. A coping saw or jigsaw is also useful for cutting square holes or scroll cuts. Use fine-tooth blades and cut so that the non-splintering side is on the good face. Saw with patience and don't force the blade.

When joining walls to a floor or base, where water may collect, cut the wall panels so that their grain runs parallel to the base. End grain will then meet vertically at the corners rather than butting against the floor where water can wick up and increase rot.

Important: Be careful to read all of the instructions to understand a project before beginning to make it.

And finally, some important tips on safety. Operate all power tools with special care. Familiarize yourself with any appropriate safety techniques such as push sticks, jigs and feather sticks. Always wear eye protection and a dust mask when cutting or sanding. Ventilate your work space properly. Use common sense, and if you're unsure about something, don't try it. If you're tired, stop.

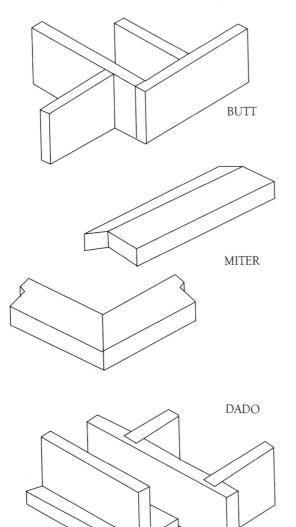

BUTT

MITER

DADO

A Versatile Mix

White Proso Millet

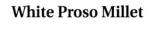

Black Striped Sunflower

Fine Cracked Corn

**Hulled Raw
Sunflower**

26

Raw Peanuts

Niger (Thistle)

Suet

Fruit Slices

Hemp Seed

27

Feeding Habits

Birds have high energy needs due to very high metabolic rates, especially the smaller species. They must eat the equivalent of between 40 and 75 percent of their body weight each day just to survive. Humans can play a very beneficial role in supplementing bird diets, particularly during severe weather such as droughts or prolonged snow cover.

The best time to start feeding birds is in early autumn. Certain flocks, like chickadees and juncos, will actually make their winter homes around good feeding areas. Because many birds will start to rely on the feed you put out, it is important to maintain your feeding program through the winter. If you must leave for awhile, taper off gradually or, better yet, ask a neighbor to take over while you're away. Come spring, providing feed is optional since natural food sources become abundant once again. There's no need to fear that birds will abandon wild foods just because they visit your feeder regularly. Providing water is a good year-round practice, though most critical during extremely cold weather.

There's not very much you can do to exclude ruffian starlings or gangs of sparrows in favor of the prettier songbirds. The best solution is to offer something to all. Set up a few different kinds of feeders, spaced apart, each with a different menu. Fill your feeders early to attract small birds like titmice, since starlings and blue jays eat later in the day. Sparrows often avoid hanging feeders. A ground feeder with inexpensive cracked corn, mixed seed or table scraps will divert many larger birds from the more expensive seed in elevated feeders.

Seeds are the most popular of feeds used to stock feeders. Although birds enjoy a great variety of seeds, which can even be mixed to suit the species in your area, sunflower seeds are the favorite of most birds. Chances are you live in a climate where you can grow your own sunflowers.

Nuts are also popular. Almost any kind will be eaten by birds, but unsalted peanuts are best. They can be strung up in their shells, mixed with other nuts in mesh bag feeders, or sprinkled almost anywhere. You'll enjoy watching nuthatches, titmice and downy woodpeckers perform their antics to get nuts hung right at your window.

Suet is hard fat trimmed from the kidneys and loins of beef or lamb. Birds love it plain during the cold months. For summer it can be rendered into "bird cakes." Melt small pieces in a pan and pour it over seeds, nuts, dried fruit, or almost any bird food, and let it cool. Or, try this alternative recipe: combine in a blender 1 part vegetable shortening, 1 part peanut butter, 1 part flour, 1 part cracked corn and 3 parts yellow corn meal. Insect-eating birds eat suet in winter when insects are scarce.

Cereal and Grain products are suitable when soaked or crumbled up for small beaks. Oats, breads, cakes, cookies, pastries, corn flakes and other variations appeal to birds.

Fruits and Vegetables such as dried peas and lentils can be served. Dried fruits such as currants and sultanas are favored by many species. Try a shish-kabob of apple, orange and other fruits to further delight bird palates.

Animal Products like small tidbits of meat, bones and cheese, along with other kitchen scraps are also worthy of bird consumption. There's almost no limit to supplementing a bird's diet.

When you opt for seed, buy in bulk. Store it in clean, dry containers with lids. Find a scoop to load your feeder, perhaps a plastic pitcher or milk jug with its bottom cut out. Clean your feeder periodically with hot water and mild detergent. Keep all feeding stations clear of old food scraps that rot and attract rats, causing infection and disease.

Feeder Fillers

White Proso Millet: Cardinals, Cowbirds, Finches (House, Chaffinch, Green Finch), Mourning Doves, Redpolls (Common), Sparrows (Field, House, White-throated), Wrens (Carolina)

Fine Cracked Corn: Blue Jays, Cardinals, Grosbeaks (Evening and Rose-breasted), Sparrows (Field, House, and others), Towhees (Green-tailed, Spotted, and Rufous-sided)

Black Oil Sunflower: American Goldfinches, Cardinals, Chickadees (Black-capped and Carolina), Grosbeaks (Evening and Rose-breasted),

Grackles (Common), Finches (House and Purple), Mourning Doves, Sparrows (Field, House, Chipping, and White-throated)

Black Striped Sunflower: Blue Jays, Cardinals, Chickadees (Black-capped and Carolina), Grosbeaks (Evening and Red-Breasted), Grackles (Common), Finches (House and Purple), Titmice (Tufted), Mourning Doves, Sparrows (House and White-throated)

Hulled Raw Sunflower: Mourning Doves, Sparrows (House)

Niger (Thistle): American

Goldfinches, Finches (House and Purple), Mourning Doves

Safflower: Cardinals

Raw Peanuts: Blue Jays, Chickadees (Black-capped and Carolina), Finches (House, Green and Purple), Goldfinches (American), Grackles (Common), Grosbeaks (Evening and Rose-breasted), Juncos, Nuthatches (Red- and White-breasted), Sparrows (Field, House and White-throated), Titmice (Tufted), Wrens (Carolina)

Suet: Blue Birds, Cardinals, Crows, Chickadees (Black-capped

and Carolina), Coal tits, Flickers, Goldfinches, Jackdaws, Juncos, Kinglets, Nuthatches (Red- and White-breasted), Thrushes, Titmice (Tufted), Warblers, Woodpeckers (Downy, Hairy, Red-bellied, Red-headed), Wrens

Fruit Slices: Blackbirds, Bluetits, Catbirds, Fieldfares, Orioles (Baltimore, Orchard, Spotted), Redwings, Robins (English), Tanagers (Scarlet, Summer, Western)

Hemp Seed: Finches (House, Chaffinch, Green Finch), Tits, Pipits

Wild Feeds

Wood Duck: Acorns, beech nuts, water plants

American Kestrel: Mainly insects, small mammals, reptiles

Northern Bobwhite: Seeds

California Quail: Seeds

Dove: Grass seeds, other seeds, and grains

Barn Owl: Rodents

Great Horned Owl: Skunks, rats, squirrels, grouse, weasels, snakes and insects

Eastern Screech Owl: Worms, crayfish, mice, small birds, insects

Chimney Swift: Flying insects

Hummingbird: Flower nectar, tree sap, some insects

Woodpecker: Acorns and other tree fruit; some insects

Flicker: Ants, insects, berries

Eastern Kingbird: Insects

Eastern Phoebe: Mainly insects

Least Flycatcher: Insects

Swallow: Mainly insects

Purple Martin: Insects

Blue Jay: Acorns, beech nuts, tree mast, insects, birds' eggs, nestlings, voles and mice

Black-billed Magpie: Insects, seeds, berries, eggs, mice, carrion

Crow: Animals, vegetables

Tufted Titmouse: Mainly insects; also seeds and berries

Bushtit and Chickadee: Mainly insects; seeds and berries

Eastern Bluebird: Insects; also berries, fruit and seeds

Western Bluebird: Insects, spiders, invertebrates; berries

Thrush: Insects, invertebrates, berries and seeds

Brown Creeper: Insects; seeds

Nuthatch: Insects, spiders, nuts, seeds and berries

Wren: Insects, invertebrates; sometimes seeds

Blue-gray Gnatcatcher: Mainly insects; other invertebrates

Kinglet: Insects, spiders and some berries

Robin: Earthworms, grubs, larvae, insects, spiders; berries, fruit, seeds

Cardinal: Mainly seeds and fruit; also insects and spiders

Mockingbird: Wild berries, seeds, insects and invertebrates

Brown Thrasher: Insects, small invertebrates, some fruit and seeds

Cedar Waxwing: Mainly berries and seeds; also insects

Warbler: Mainly insects and spiders; sometimes seeds and berries

Yellowthroat: Insects

American Redstart: Insects, spiders, fruit and seeds

Grosbeak: Insects and fruit; seeds and berries

Bunting: Insects, spiders, berries and seeds

Towhee: Seeds, fruit and insects

Dark-eyed Junco: Mainly insects and seeds

Finch: Mainly seeds and fruit; also insects

Oriole: Mainly insects and spiders; also fruit and seeds

Brown-headed Cowbird: Grain, seeds, berries and other fruit; some insects

Common Grackle: Insects, grass seeds, worms, eggs and young birds

Eastern Meadowlark: Insects, grubs, grass and weed seeds

Blackbird: Insects and seeds

Sparrow: Insects, seeds and fruit

Red Crossbill: Pine seeds, other fruit and seeds

Pine Siskin: Seeds and some insects

Common Redpoll: Mainly insects and fruit

"Everyone Needs a Home" (series) by
Don Bundrick

"Boyds in the 'Hood" by Don Bundrick

Three ***Bird Houses*** by Marshall Fall

"Cross Birdhouses" (series) by Charles Ratliff

Gallery

Three *"Gourd Houses"* by Harold Hall

Opposite, *"Lighthouse"* by Fox Watson & the students at Juvenile Evaluation Center, Swannanoa, NC

"Bluebird House"
by Paul Sumner

Three *"Nuthatch Houses"* by Paul Sumner

Bird Houses by Susan Starr

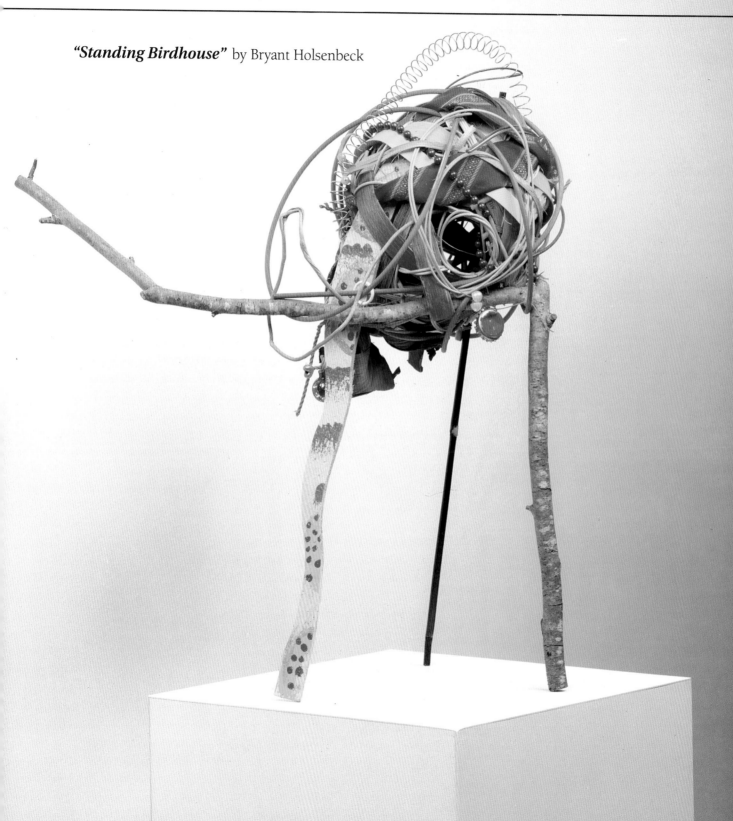

"Standing Birdhouse" by Bryant Holsenbeck

"A-Frame Birdhouse" (front and back views) by Bobby Hansson

Bird Houses by Barry Leader

40

Bird Baths by Debra Fritts
(Photos by Sue Ann Kuhn-Smith)

"If That Mockingbird Don't Sing" (left and detail) and *"Nature Gets The Exxit"* (middle) by Mana D. C. Hewitt

"Closed Doors" (open and closed)
by Mana D. C. Hewitt

"Global View" (open and closed)
by Mana D. C. Hewitt

"Ironclad Monitor" by Randy Sewell

"Tar Paper Fishing Shack"
by Randy Sewell

"Oasis" by Randy Sewell

"Radio World"
by Randy Sewell

"Java Jive" by Randy Sewell

"Silo Birdfeeder"
by Randy Sewell

"Lewis' Reptile Farm"
by Randy Sewell

Wall Feeder & Bath by Carol Costenbader

Amorphous Environ by David Renfroe

"Sunflower Birdhouse" by West Olive Folk Art

"Country Bird Feeder"
by Bruce Malicoat

Twig Tent Feeder

What could be more simple—an A-frame roof over a feeding platform. The materials and construction may vary, but they're all within reach and easy to assemble. This is a great way to start feeding—and watching—birds.

Feeders

Mosaic Twig Feeder

Once you get the knack of splitting twigs, the possibilities for mosaic ornamentation are endless. This wall-mounted feeder discourages squirrels and mice, yet is easily refilled to attract all sorts of birds.

Twig Tent Feeder

Materials List

	1 x 12 x 12" Pine base
2	1-1/4" dia. x 12" Twigs
1 or 2	16" V-shaped twigs
	1" dia. x 9" Twig
3–4	Coffee cans
	Bundle of broom corn
6	1-3/4" Wood screws
	Twine
	Glue and assorted nails

Step One You can saw one V-shaped twig in half, or use two the same size, for the roof frame. They are glued and screwed to the base from the bottom. The 9" twig is glued and screwed between both apexes to form the roof ridge.

Step Two Saw the two 12" twigs in half, then glue and nail them around the edge of the base to form a lip for the feed tray.

Step Three Open and flatten coffee can barrels, then nail them over the roof frame, overlapping the peak. For a more natural look, tie broom corn over these tin panels with twine. This can be replaced as the birds eat the broom corn seeds. Mount this feeder on a post.

Mosaic Twig Feeder

Materials List

2	1 x 12 x 12" Pine
	1 x 8" x 10" Pine
2	10" V-shaped twigs
	1" dia. x 9" Twig
	1-1/4" dia. x 12" Twig
	1" dia. x 12" Twig
	1-1/4" dia. x 8" Twig
	1/4"–3/8" Assorted Twigs
	Juice can
	Large hinge
2	4" Steel L-brackets
6	1-3/4" Wood screws
	Glue and assorted nails

Step One The 8" x 10" base and V-shaped uprights are joined in the same manner as the previous feeder. The 9" twig is screwed to the apexes of the uprights. The 8" twig is split in half, then glued and nailed to the side edges of the base. The 1-1/4" x 12" twig is split, and half is attached to the front edge of the base to complete the lip.

Step Two The juice can is opened at the top end, then punctured with a can opener around the bottom edge of the cylinder to spill seed. It is screwed to the center of the base. The base assembly is then attached to the bottom edge of one of the 12 x 12" panels with glue and nails. It is reinforced with two L-brackets.

Step Three The other half of the 1-1/4" x 12" twig is glued and nailed to the front edge of the roof. The 1" x 12" twig is split for the side edges. Trace a pattern on the roof panel. Split the assorted twigs with a hunting knife and mallet for the mosaic. The smallest twigs may be left whole. Those to be bent can be boiled first. Cut each to the appropriate length, then predrill and nail them into the pattern. The roof will be hinged to the back.

Bark-Faced Feeder

This classic design has been embellished with a woodsy mix of twigs, mosses and lichens. It is a highly functional feeder that will attract frequent flyers, and it's easy to make.

Materials List

> 1 x 5" x 7" Pine base
> 6-1/2" x 10-1/2" Bark-faced slab
> 2 1-1/4" dia. x 5" Twigs
> 2 2" x 11" Bark-faced slabs
> 2 2" x 5" Bark-faced slabs
> 4 #10 Wood screws
> Eyescrew
> Glues and assorted nails

Step One Glue and nail the two 2" x 5" slabs to the 5" edges of the base, flush at bottom. Glue and nail the two 2" x 11" slabs to the long edges of the base, completing the feed tray.

Step Two Glue the two 5" posts to each end of the base, reinforcing with screws from the underside. Glue and top screw the roof slab to the posts. Install the eyescrew top center.

Step Three Attach all the woodsy ornamentation with clear silicone sealant.

Thatched Twig Feeder

Here's yet another variation using all natural materials. This post-mounted feeding pavilion features a thatched roof with ornamental wattle railings and sub-roofing.

Materials List

> 8" x 16" Log slab
> 4 1/2" dia. x 12" Forked branches
> Lots of assorted twigs
> 3 1" dia. x 17" Twigs
> Bundle of straw
> Tie wire
> Glue

Step One Trim 1" of bark off the non-forked end of each post branch. Drill slanted 1/2" holes for these four corner posts into the log slab, about 5" and 10" apart. Glue the posts into place, rotating the forked tops to accept the roof frame.

Step Two Attach four main twig members to the forked post tops with tie wire. The smaller end members should be V-shaped to form a roof peak. Attach smaller V-shaped cross pieces to the longer side members with tie wire. Weave the smaller twigs lengthwise through these cross pieces to form a peaked roof frame.

Step Three Insert 3/8" dia. x 10-1/2" twigs into pre-drilled and glued holes in the corner posts for two pairs of top and bottom rails. Wire on a few upright slats, then weave smaller twigs through these to form wattled railings. The upright slats could also be pre-drilled and glued into the railings.

Step Four The thatched straw is wired to the wattled roof frame. Lacquer it thoroughly for longer life. Split the 17" twigs that will be wired through the thatch to the frame to form the roof ridge and eaves caps. Add whatever ornamental bracing and decoration you like with more twigs.

Bird Cage Feeder

Grapevines are a wonderful material to make this charming cage, complete with trapeze. See how many pretty birds try out the swing, swoop down for a tempting morsel, then fly the coop, evading jailbird captivity.

Materials List

An armful of grapevines
A small spool of tie wire
8" dia. Plastic tray (potted
*   plant saucer)*
Side cutters

In place of grapevines, you can use willow or other flexible material. Tie wire can be found at most any lumber yard or hardware store.

Step One Roll grapevines into circles A, B, C and F as shown.

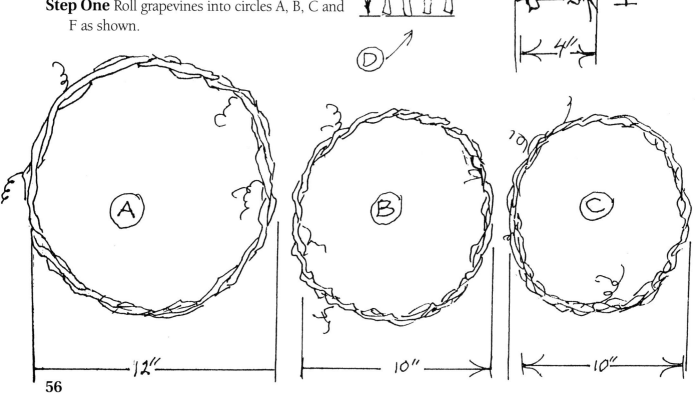

Step Two Wire four
bottom bars E
with tie wire to C.

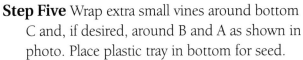

Step Three Wire 42" D bars to *inside* of C at
joints of C and E. Install only 2 D bars as
shown.

Step Four Place B inside D bars 4" from C. Cage
bottom wire in place, then insert A 11" from
bottom and wire in place.

Step Five Wrap extra small vines around bottom
C and, if desired, around B and A as shown in
photo. Place plastic tray in bottom for seed.

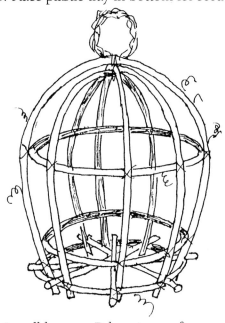

Step Six Install last two D bars just as first two
were installed. Wire F circle to top, and hang
swing inside center.

Traditional Slant

Here's a new slant on a classic birdfeeder design, fashioned out of durable cedar. It's fun to make, and features a clever lift-off roof panel for easy feed loading.

Materials List

2 *1 x 7-1/4" x 18-1/4" Cedar*
2 *1 x 7-1/4" x 17-1/2" Cedar*
   1 x 7-1/4" x 5-3/4" Cedar
3 *1 x 2-1/2" x 4-1/4" Cedar*
   1 x 2" x 4-1/4" Cedar
2 *1 x 1" x 5-3/4" Cedar*
2 *1/2" x 1-3/4" x 10-1/8" Cedar*
2 *5/16" x 6-1/8" Dowels*
2 *3-1/4" x 4-5/8" Plexiglass*
   4" x 9-1/4" Copper flashing
2 *Rubber bumper knobs*
   Glue and assorted nails

Step One Cut a 45° bevel on each upper corner of the 1/2" cedar pieces. Drill a 5/16" hole, 1/4" deep, below each bevel. Insert the dowels with glue as you glue and nail the 1/2" stock, centered and flush at the bottom, to the 5-3/4" x 7-1/4" base plate.

Step Two Rip cut a 45° bevel on the two 1 x 1" strips. Glue and nail these pieces on the open edges of the base to complete the feeding tray.

Step Three Rip cut intersecting 75° bevels on one long edge of two of the three 2-1/2" x 4-1/4" blocks. One of these will be affixed to the removable roof panel. The other supports the two spear-shaped walls, along with the square block opposite, just above the plexiglass slot. Rip cut 45° bevels on the two top long edges of the 2" x 4-1/4" base block.

Step Four Cut the two spear-shaped walls from the 17-1/2" lengths of cedar. Cut a 1/4" deep groove in both lower slanted edges of each wall. Glue and nail the walls to the two side blocks and base block as shown in the drawing. Attach the rubber knobs to the base bevels, then insert the plexiglass. This assembly can now be inserted into the center of the feeding tray, and glued and nailed in place.

Step Five Rip cut a 15° bevel off one short edge of each 18-1/4" roof panel to intersect as a peak. Place both panels in position, remove the fixed side, then mark the position of the upper beveled block to be attached to the removable panel. Glue and nail the block in place.

Step Six Put both panels back in position, and glue and nail the fixed side. Bend the copper in half lengthwise, then lay it over the roof peak. Bend, clip and crimp the ends, then nail them to the removable panel.

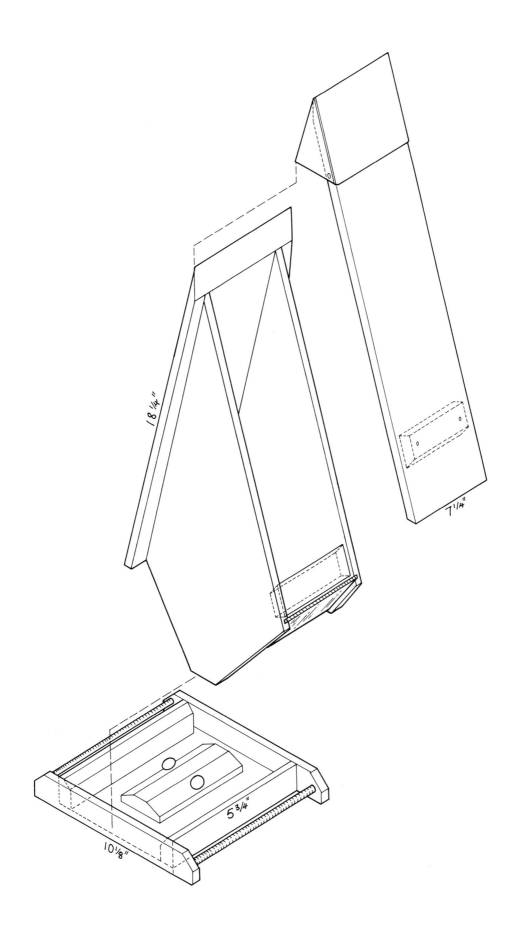

18 1/4"

7 1/4"

5 3/4"

10 1/8"

Pyramid Canopy

So elegant and simple, this redwood and copper feeder needs no glue or fasteners. The brass chain does all the work. Just hang it, fill it, and watch the birds feed.

Materials List

3	*1 x 9-1/2" x 11-1/4" Redwood*
	12" x 13" Copper flashing
2	*1/2" Split key rings*
5	*7/8" Brass S hooks*
6	*5/8" Brass S hooks*
6	*Brass eyescrews*
3	*8-1/2" Brass chains*
3	*4" Brass chains*

Step One Straight cut the 90° notch 1-3/4" into one long edge of each redwood block. Mark another 90° angle from the center of the opposite long edge. Undercut 35° bevels along each diagonal line. Drill a 1/4" hole in each roof panel centered near the apex. (See Diagram 1.)

Step Two Cut a triangle with flanges from the copper flashing. (See Diagram 2.) Fold along the dotted lines to create a triangular tray with double thick rims. Drill 1/16" holes through the double thick upper corners of each rim.

Step Three If you wish to glue the roof sections together, do so now. However, the sections will hang neatly in place without glue once the chains are installed.

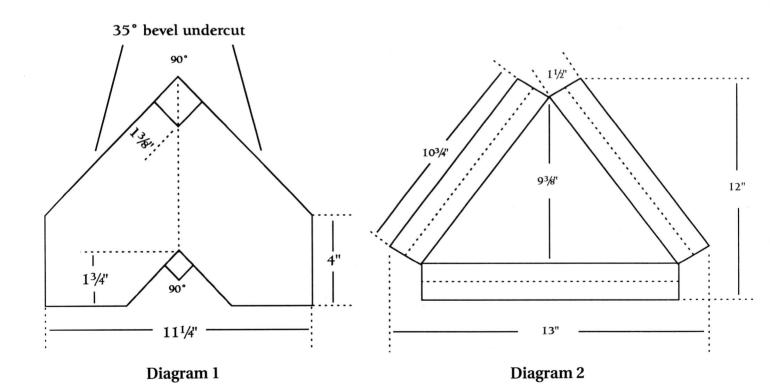

Diagram 1   **Diagram 2**

Step Four On the inside surface of the roof panels, pre-drill and insert eyescrews 5/8" in from each edge of the bottom outside corners. Insert and crimp a 5/8" S hook through each of the six corner holes in the copper tray. Insert and crimp a 7/8" S hook through each of these smaller pairs of S hooks. Open both end links of the 4" chains, hook them on each pair of eyescrews, then crimp them closed. Insert the top of each large S hook through the center link of each chain and crimp it closed.

Step Five Join one end of each 8-1/2" chain with a split ring. Pass one chain through each roof hole from the underside. Insert and crimp an S hook through the other end of each chain. Add another S hook to this one. Suspend the structure from this top S hook. Pass a split ring through each chain 1/2" above the apex of the roof, or join them with single chain links (as in the photo).

Plentiful Pagoda

Three tiers of tempting treats await your famished feathered friends. With an oriental flare, this ingenious design features top-loaded feed that trickles down to fill all levels.

Materials List

> 3/4" x 17" x 17" Plywood
> 1/2" x 12-5/16" x 12-5/16" Plywood
> 1/2" x 7-15/16" x 7-15/16" Plywood
> 1/2" x 3-13/16" x 3-13/16" Plywood
> 4   1/2" x 7" x 13" Plywood
> 4   1/2" x 6" x 8-5/8" Plywood
> 4   1/2" x 6" x 4-1/2" Plywood
> 4   1/4" x 1-1/2" x 17-1/2" Cedar
> 4   5/8" x 4-5/8" x 18" Cedar
> 4   5/8" x 3-3/8" x 12-1/4" Cedar
> 4   5/8" x 3-3/8" x 8-1/4" Cedar
> 4   5/8" x 3-5/8" x 4-1/2" Cedar
> Glues and assorted finishing nails

Step One In each corner of the 3/4" plywood base, drill a 1/2" drainage hole centered 1" from each edge. Measure 7" from each corner toward the center, and drill four more 1/2" drainage holes. You may wish to cover each hole with a 1" circle of window screen, which you can affix with clear silicone.

Step Two Miter cut all the short edges of the 7" x 13" wall panels for corner joints. Rip cut a 37-1/2° bevel along one long edge of each panel for roof joints. Dado cut a 1/2" groove, 3/16" deep, 1" from the top on the non-beveled side. Using a hole saw, cut three equidistant 2" holes centered 1-1/4" up from the bottom edge of each panel. (The holes need to be lower than those pictured.)

Step Three Centered 1" from each edge of the 12-5/16" square, drill 1-1/4" holes in each corner, then four more between these. Centered 1" from each edge of the 7-15/16" square, drill 1-1/4" holes in each corner, then a fifth hole in the center. Drill a 3" hole in the center of the 3-13/16" square. Cut the remaining wall panels in the same manner as the bottom tier, with 2" holes centered 1-1/4" from the bottom edge.

Step Four Using glue and nails, join the top four wall panels, inserting the 3-13/16" square into the dadoed groove at the top. Let dry, then glue and nail this assembly to the center of the 7-15/16" square. Join the middle tier of walls, inserting the top assembly into the groove. Let dry, then glue and nail this assembly to the center of the next larger square, and so on down to the bottom. Varnish this plywood assembly thoroughly before attaching the cedar roof panels.

Step Five Mark a 55° line from each bottom corner of all cedar roof panels to form the trapezoids. The top cap sections will be triangles. Set your table saw blade at 52-1/2°, and cut along each of these lines. Each tier is then glued into place, nailing the top edges into the wall bevels, and angle nailing the bottom corners to reinforce the seams. You can use clear silicone in place of glue for durable roof seams.

Step Six You may wish to bevel the 1/4" cedar lath for the tapered look shown here. Miter the corners, then glue and nail each strip to form the lip of the foundation.

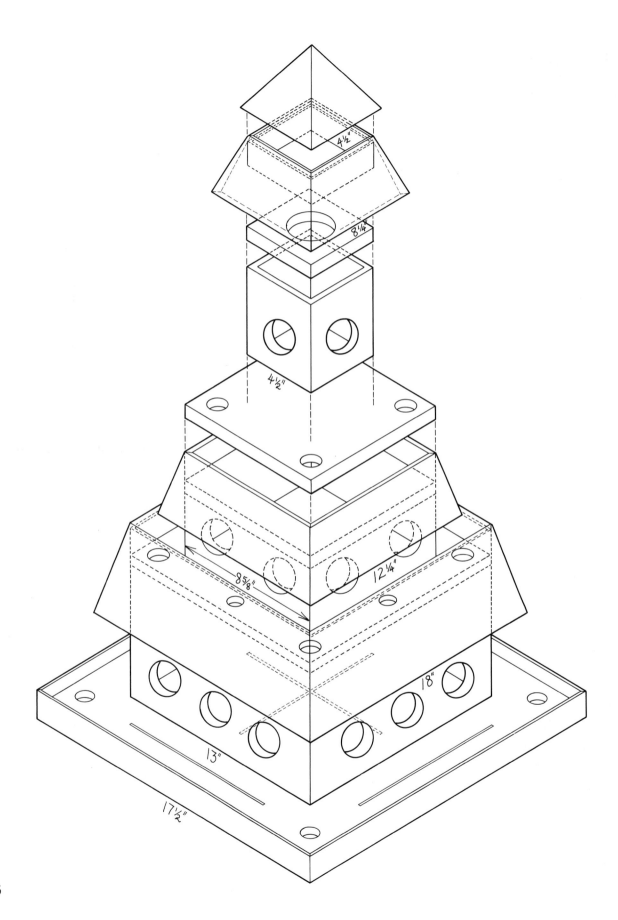

English Country Gazebo

This Old World way station for hungry birds has natural appeal as a landscaping ornament. The hexagonal, double-roofed pavilion can be made of cedar, redwood or pine, then left to weather.

Materials List

2   1 x 9" x 20" Solid stock
6   1 x 5" x 11" Solid stock
6   5/8" x 1-1/2" x 9-3/4" Solid stock
6   5-1/2" x 11-1/4" x 11-3/4" Triangles of 1/2" solid stock
6   4" x 7-1/2" x 7-1/2" Triangles of 1/2" solid stock
     3/8" Solid stock scrap
     Glue and assorted nails

Step One Lay the two base planks side by side, then trace a hexagon with 9-3/4" sides that fills the area. Cut off the outside corners.

Step Two Miter cut both long edges of all six 5" x 11" wall panels at 60° to form the hexagonal chamber. Using a jigsaw, cut the arched window openings in each panel. The bottom sill is centered 2-1/4" from each bottom edge. The openings measure 2-1/4" x 6".

Step Three Join the six walls with glue or clear silicone. Use large rubber bands to hold them together while they dry. Small brads can be tapped in to reinforce the seams after the glue is dry.

Step Four Apply glue to the bottom rim of the chamber as well as the center seam of the base planks, assemble upside down and top nail the base to the chamber. Then pre-drill and add wood screws for reinforcement. Let dry.

Step Five Miter cut the 9-3/4" rail section at 60° Drill 1/2" holes through the center lengthwise for decoration. Glue the adjoining edges, then nail into place. By inverting the structure, you can lay the base over the rails and top nail them. Angled corner nails will reinforce the corner seams.

Step Six All twelve roof sections will need to be miter cut at 52-1/2° along intersecting edges to form the hexagonal cones. Join them by applying a large bead of glue or silicone to each seam, then leaning the sections together and pressing them into alignment. Let dry, then sand the seams smooth. The eaves can be trimmed neatly after joining. Each roof section can be glued and nailed into place. You may also wish to add a decorative spire. The stem should be inserted and glued into the apex.

Step Seven Cut the six arch-shaped stoops from the 3/8" stock. They should measure 2" x 4". They are simply glued and nailed onto the sills.

Step Eight Cut the window trim from solid 3/8" stock. They will measure 3-1/2" x 7-1/2" before cutting. You can gang half or all at the same time depending on whether you use a band saw, a jigsaw or coping saw. Use glue and small brads to secure them in place.

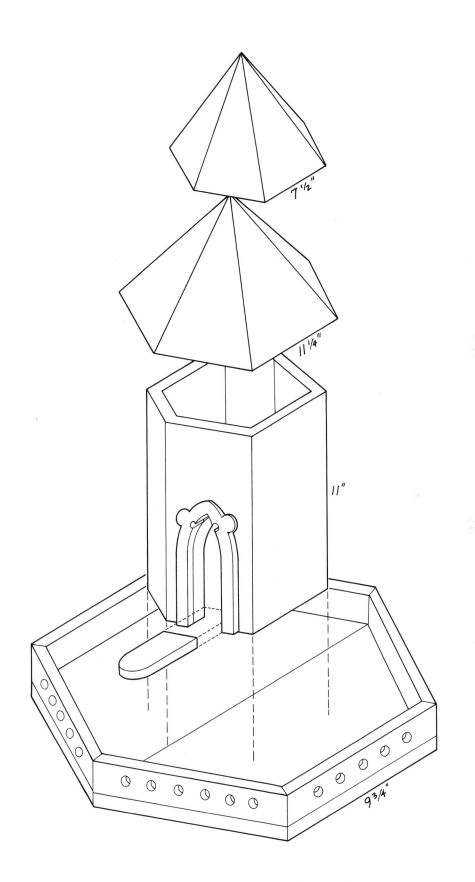

7 1/2"

11 1/4"

11"

9 3/4"

69

Wishing Well

This nostalgic feeder exudes country charm, and it can be constructed many ways—from a rustic romp to a cooper's dream. No matter, a bird's only wish will be that you keep it well stocked.

Materials List

	1/2" x 6-3/4" dia. Plywood
	1/4" x 11-1/4" dia. Plywood
12	*1/2" x 2" x 4" Pine*
2	*3/4" x 3/4" x 11" Pine*
	1-1/2" x 1-1/2" dia. Dowel
	1 x Scrap
	1/4" Scrap
	1/4" x 10" Dowel
	5-1/2" Metal rod
	8" Nylon string
	1-1/2" dia. Wooden spool
	5-1/2" Heavy wire
	Large eyescrew
2	*#8 Wood screws*
	1-1/4" dia. Screen
	Glue and assorted nails

The well shown here is basically a cylindrical bucket with a conical roof. This can be constructed using various materials and techniques. It could also be a square or polygonal shape. The structure could even be purchased ready-made. It's entirely up to you.

Step One Find some reasonably tight-grained or furniture grade stock for the bucket slats. The 2" x 4" pieces will need to be bevel cut on the long sides at 30°. Using large rubber bands or a circular clamp, glue these slats together into a cylindrical barrel shape. Let dry.

Step Two The bucket shown here was taper cut on a machinist's lathe. All you need to do with your polygon is round off the exterior. You can whittle before sanding if you want it really rounded. Also sand the top and bottom rims.

Step Three Cut the floor of the bucket to fit snugly after tracing the interior shape onto the 1/2" plywood. Wedge into the bottom with glue and tack it in place. Cut a 3/8" hole in the center, then glue or tack the screen over it for drainage.

Step Four The two 3/4" support posts are glued to the sides, nailed at the bottom, and screwed from the inside bucket rim. You may want to notch them as in the photo. If your bucket is tapered, the top should be beveled slightly to join with the roof disk. Drill a 1/4" hole halfway into one post, 1-1/2" from the top, before joining. Glue and nail the roof disk to the posts.

Step Five Taper the 1-1/2" dowel at the top before gluing it to the center of the 11-1/4" plywood disk. Cut triangles from the 1 x and 1/4" scrap. Glue the 1 x triangles like spokes around the tapered dowel (see photo). Layer the triangular 1/4" shingles over this substructure with glue. Let dry, then insert the eyescrew at the apex.

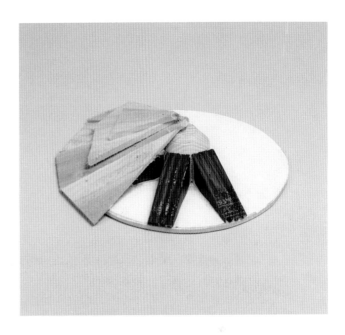

Step Six Cut the 10" dowel into a 9-1/4" shaft and a 3/4" handle. Drill holes into one end of each to accommodate the metal rod. Bend the rod into a crankshaft, then glue it into both dowels. Drill a 1/4" hole through the undrilled post, 1-1/2" from the top, then insert the shaft. You may glue it in place, or leave it free to turn.

Step Seven The bucket shown here was lathe-turned. You can make a reasonable facsimile from a wooden spool, or purchase one from a hobby store in the doll house department. The 5-1/2" wire handle is bent and inserted into pre-drilled holes. Tie the nylon string to the shaft, wrap it, then dangle it to tie onto the bucket handle. Stain the assembly to your taste.

Covered Bridge

These quaint country crossings may be disappearing from rural landscapes, but they're due for a revival in bird feeder architecture. This perfectly adapted design will experience heavy traffic from birds on the wing, and built out of cedar, may last as long as its predecessor.

Materials List

2   *1 x 7-5/8" x 27" Cedar*
     1 x 7" x 24" Cedar
2   *1 x 7" x 8-5/8" Cedar*
2   *1 x 2-1/2" x 8-1/2" Cedar*
     1 x 4" x 4" Cedar
     1-1/2" x 1-1/2" x 6' Cedar post
4   *1/2" x 1/2" x 22-5/8" Cedar*
2   *1/2" x 1/2" x 5" Cedar*
28   *1/4" x 1-1/2" Dowels*
     Cedar shake shingles
4   *#10 Wood screws*
8   *#8 Wood screws*
     Glues and assorted nails

Step One Rip cut 45° tapered bevels on all long edges of the two 27" roof panels. Cut the 45° roof peak and rounded arch out of both 7" x 8-5/8" blocks at once. Mark the arch with a compass.

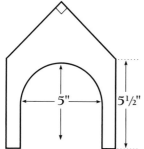

Step Two Drill fourteen 1/4" holes along one face of each 22-5/8" rail. They should match up on 1-1/2" centers and be 1/4" deep. Rub glue around each dowel tip before tapping it into the bottom rails. Rub glue on the upper tips before tapping the top rails onto them. Let dry.

Step Three Glue and nail the rails to the arch blocks to form the walls. They should be flush at the bottom and at the corners. Let dry.

Step Four Glue this assembly to the 24" base, clamping or weighting for tight seams. After seams are dry, reinforce the arches with four #8 screws from the underside corners. Glue and nail the 5" lip molding inside the arch thresholds.

Step Five Using clear silicone sealant, glue both roof panels atop the arches. After seams are dry, reinforce the roof to arch seams by top nailing. The shingles are attached one row at a time from the bottom, also using silicone. If you use non-cedar shingles, such as available for doll houses, you should add two coats of polyurethane to protect them.

Step Six Cut both scalloped braces from the 2-1/2" x 8-1/2" pieces at the same time on a band saw or jigsaw. Cut a decorative bevel on the edges of the 4" square post block.

Step Seven Attach the post block, bevels down, to one end of the post with two #8 screws. Attach the block to the center of the base with two #8 screws. Attach both scalloped braces to base and post with countersunk #10 screws.

Cascading Post

This modern design sports multi-level feeding decks that Frank Lloyd Wright might have engineered. The top-loaded feed spirals down around the post, and it's all under one roof. An intriguing blend of function and aesthetics.

Materials List

	3-3/4" x 3-3/4" x 5" Pine block
4	1/4" x 4" x 16" Plywood walls
	1/4" x 3-3/4" x 10-1/8" Plywood partition
	1/4" x 14" x 14" Plywood roof
2	1/4" x 8" x 8" Plywood decks
2	1/4" x 4" x 6" Plywood braces
	1/4" x 2-1/8" x 3-3/4" Plywood floor
4	1/4" x 7/8" x 8-1/4" Plywood
4	1/4" x 7/8" x 4-1/4" Plywood
2	1-1/2" Threaded posts
2	Matching capped nuts
	Glues and nails

Step One It should be noted that this entire structure can be built around a pressure-treated 4 x 4 post, the upper 5" of which would be encased. A squirrel barrier would then be advisable. Also, you are encouraged to substitute solid 1/4" stock in place of plywood if you can find it. This is not crucial so long as you thoroughly caulk, prime and paint the plywood structure to withstand the elements.

Step Two If you are not building this around a 4 x 4 post, procure a 1" steel pipe (threaded at the top end), and cut a snug hole in the bottom center of the pine block.

Step Three Cut 22-1/2° angles across the tops of the wall panels. In one of these panels, cut a 5/8" x 3" slot, the sill of which is centered 5" up from the straight bottom. In another panel, cut the same slot 11" above the straight bottom edge.

Step Four Wood glue and rubber bands (for clamping) will be used to join the walls around the pine block, with successive butt joints. However, as you join these, you must also glue in place the central partition as well as the 2-1/8" x 3-3/4" floor of the upper chamber (see drawing). You may wish to pre-glue the floor and partition assembly. Note that the partition is aligned off-center toward the lower chamber, and rests on the pine block inside the four walls. The walls should be turned so that the bevels alternate, creating two planes for the peaked roof. Sand all surfaces flat and square with a sanding block before joining.

Step Five Cut a V-slot 7/8" in from each corner on the long edge of the two 4" x 6" pieces. These K-shaped braces will support the decks. (Rather than joining these separate pieces to the main trunk chamber, you could cut the two non-slotted walls to include this irregular shape intact.)

Step Six Cut the 4" x 4" upper decks out of one corner of the two 8" x 8" deck pieces. Cut all eight 7/8" strips that form the lips of the decks. Sand all of these surfaces flat and square.

Step Seven Glue one pair of decks at a time. Lay the trunk chamber horizontally each time and add weights to all appropriate members so that all seams dry tightly. Sand the seams of the entire assembly once it has dried.

Step Eight Cut the 14" square roof panel diagonally with a 52-1/2° beveled angle. Using

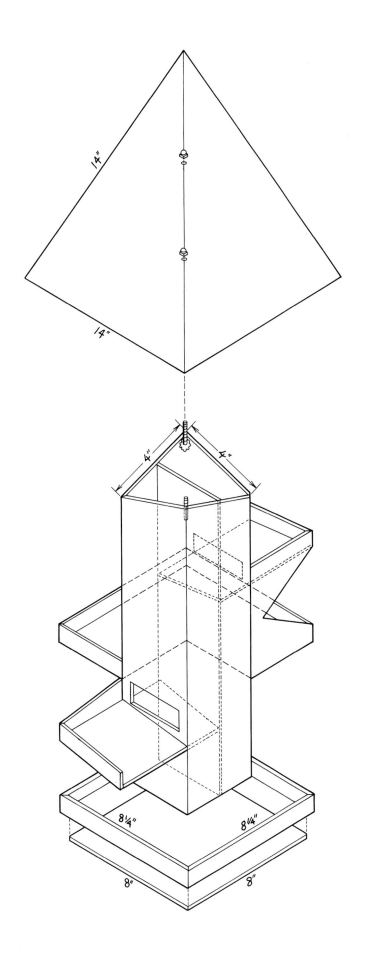

shims to support these angled panels, glue them together along the long beveled seam. (You can glue a triangular block into the center if you wish to brace them.)

Step Nine Epoxy the two threaded posts inside the opposite high corners of the trunk chamber. They should extend 1/2" above the corner rim.

Step Ten Lay the roof over the center of the trunk chamber. Carefully mark the points where the threaded posts meet the underside ridge. Drill snug holes to accommodate the posts.

Step Eleven Thoroughly caulk, prime and paint the structure according to your own taste.

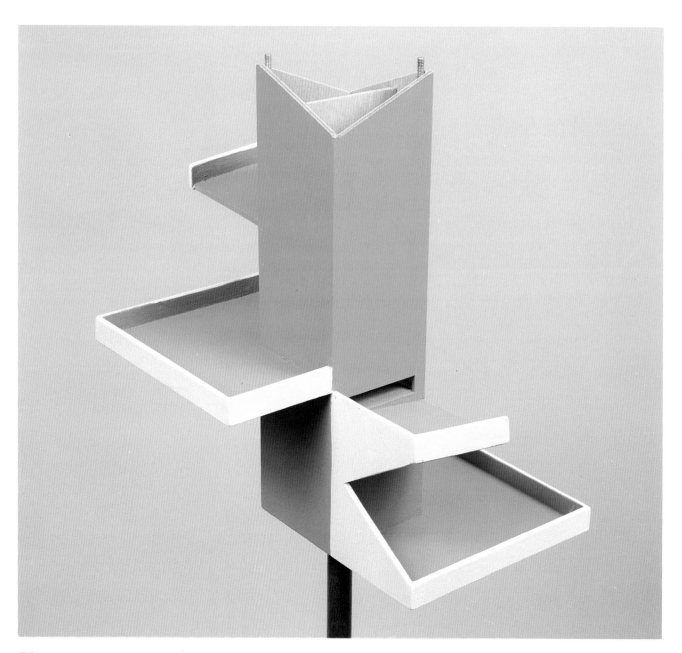

Birdie Can-teen

A child can make this simple feeder with hand tools and minimal supervision. And in addition, it is a very functional feeder that can be decorated many different ways.

Materials List

	1 x 11-1/4" x 11-1/4" Pine
	1 x 7-7/8" x 7-7/8" Pine
4	1/4" x 1-1/2" x 8-3/16" Lath
	3-7/8" Dia. coffee can
	16' Clothes line
2	#6 Wood screws
	Glue and assorted nails

Step One The pine squares can be cut with a hand saw. Find the center point in both pine squares. Mark two points in each, 3" apart in the center and parallel with each other, and drill 1/4" holes in all four points.

Step Two The lath can be glued and nailed in successive butt joints around the base, flush with the bottom, or mitered from 8-7/8" lengths if you prefer.

Step Three Cut four openings in one end of the can with a can opener, hammering back the triangular flap with a screwdriver and hammer flush with the can's bottom. The top should be removed.

Step Four Paint the can and both plates as you wish. Let dry. Screw the can to the center of the bottom plate from the top, punching holes in the can with a nail and hammer near the perimeter of the circle.

Step Five Run the clothes line (preferably plastic coated, to defy squirrel traction) in a long U shape through the top, into the can and through a bottom hole, back up through the other bottom hole and through the top. This can be hung from a big tree or other high places.

Bird Feeder

This bird likes nothing better than to hang around and feed her fellow fowls. They will visit often to perch on her wings and sample the fruit or bread scraps *du jour*.

Materials List

    1 x 3-1/4" x 9-1/2" Pine

2   *3/8" x 2-3/4" x 8" Pine*

    3/8" x 2-3/4" x 3-1/2" Pine

3   *1-1/2" Nails*

    Eyescrew

    Glue

Step One With a coping, jig or band saw, cut the outlines of the body, wings and tail as shown in the photos, or as you prefer. Whittle the edges into pleasing tapers, except where the wings and tail will join the body.

Step Two On a table or band saw, cut a 3/8" notch into the body's tail about 1" deep. With a coping or jig saw, cut a 3/8" x 1-1/2" slot through the belly area. Whittle and sand these junctures until all pieces fit snugly. Glue them in place and let dry. Whittle and sand the tail joint.

Step Three Prime and paint the bird as you wish with outdoor paint. This bird has an antique finish. Keep in mind that you may want to wash the bird periodically.

Step Four Using a same size nail, drill holes into the top of the body as shown in the photo. Snip the heads off three nails and glue them into these holes with epoxy. Install the eyescrew wherever the piece will balance with food spiked on it.

Cardinal Dispensation

They say that gluttony is a cardinal sin. See how often you have to refill this tempting see-through feeder, and you may discern which is nobler: man or bird.

Materials List

2	*2 x 9" x 10" Pine*
	1 x 4-1/2" x 4-1/2" Pine
4	*1/4" x 1-1/2" x 4-5/8" Lath*
2	*4-1/2" x 5-3/8" Plexiglass*
	Sink stopper
	Eyescrew
	Glue and assorted nails
	Clear silicone sealant

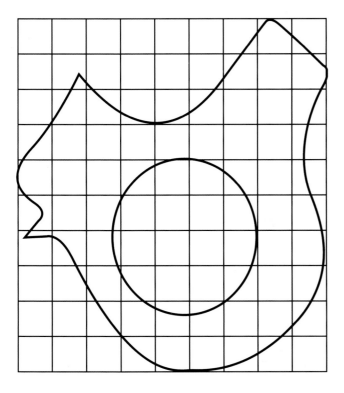

Step One Trace a bird pattern on one of the 2 x pine blocks. Cut it out with a jig or band saw. If you have access to a hole saw, cut a 4-1/4" circle out of the center. Otherwise, trace and cut the circle with a jig or band saw. The bottom of the circle should be 1-3/4" from the bottom edge of the bird.

Step Two Lay this cut piece on top of the other 2 x pine block, then trace the circle and the outline. Cut this block to match. Glue and clamp them together. Let dry, then sand the seams smooth.

Step Three Lay a plexiglass rectangle over one of the holes, leaving a 3/8" opening for seed spill. Trace a C-shaped outline around the hole that has a 5/8" margin. Cut this shape gently with a fine tooth coping saw. Trace and cut the other pane the same.

Step Four Cut the 1 x pine square diagonally into two triangles. Miter cut the short edges of the lath, then glue and nail them to the short sides of both triangles, flush with the bottoms. Glue and nail these wings to the body, with the top surface flush with the circle bottoms. Let dry.

Step Five Using a hole saw or coping saw, cut a hole in the top of the bird through to the feed chamber, big enough to accept the sink stopper snugly.

Step Six Paint the entire assembly to taste. Topcoat with a sealant to preserve the center glue seam.

Step Seven Pre-drill the nail holes through the plexiglass. Run a bead of silicone around the curved edges, then nail them into place. Install the eyescrew.

Catfish Windvane

Reminiscent of primitive American folk art, this whimsical windvane features a unique advantage in bird feeding comfort. No matter which way the wind is blowing, the cat's head always shelters our dainty diners from the elements.

Materials List

	1 x 12 x 28" Pine
2	*1 x 5-1/2" x 6-1/2" Pine*
	1 x 7-1/2" x 8-1/4" Pine
	1 x 5-1/2" x 8-1/4" Pine
	1 x 4-1/4" x 4-1/4" Pine
	1/4" dia. x 1-1/2" x 8" Lath
	5' Heavy wire
2	*2" Lag screws*
	16d Nail
	1-1/4" dia. x 6'–8' Post
	Glue and assorted nails

Step One First, build the head. Cut 80° bevels around the 4-1/4" x 4-1/4" face block to join with the flared sides. The face surface will then measure about 4" square.

Step Two Mark points on both 5-1/2" x 6-1/2" side blocks, 1-1/4" in from each corner on the same long edge. Draw lines from these points to the opposite corners, then cut along these lines at 90°. Bevel the 4" edge at 80° on both blocks.

Step Three Mark points on the 5-1/2" x 8-1/4" bottom block, 1-3/8" in from each corner on the same long edge. Draw lines from these points to the opposite corners, then cut along these lines at 90°. Trace this shape onto the 7-1/2" x 8-1/4" top block, with the 5-1/2" edge

flush with one 7-1/2" edge. Trace and cut at 90°. Bevel the 5-1/2" edges of both blocks at 80°. (The overhang on the top block is a rain-shed.)

Step Four Glue and nail the head together. Let dry, then sand all the seams. Using a coping or jigsaw, cut wavy lines along the outer edges of the top and sides to suggest tufts of fur.

Step Five Using a jig or band saw, cut a fish body outline from the 28" board. Save the scrap. A tapered neck area should extend about 4". The bottom edge of the neck must be flat to join with the head, and angled parallel to ground level. A hole, slightly larger than the 16d nail should be drilled about 2" deep, perpendicular to the bottom neck edge. This will keep the feed tray level.

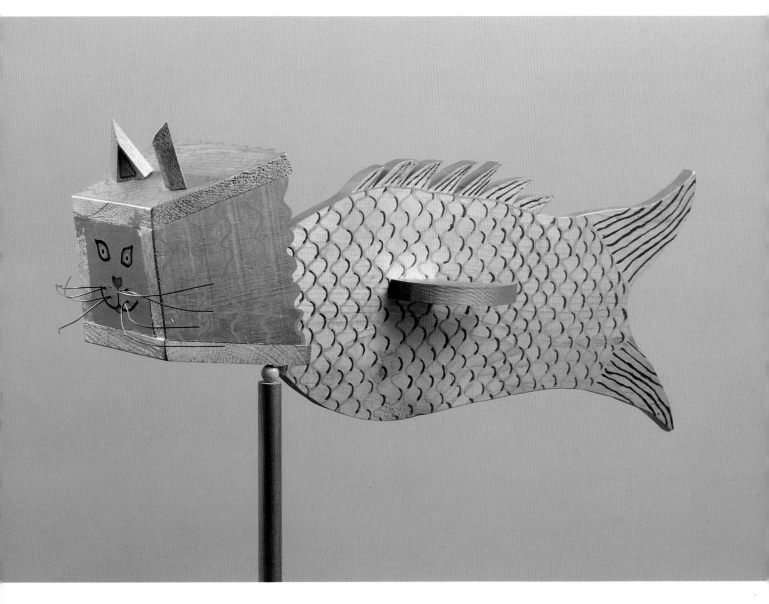

Step Six Cut curved side fins from the scrap, then glue and nail them to the body. Bevel cut two triangles to make ears about 2-1/2" tall. Glue and nail them on.

Step Seven Glue and nail the neck into the head. Reinforce this joint with two 2" lag screws from the underside of the head. Cut the lath into two 4" lengths. Glue and tack these to the bottom edge of the head, forming a lip for the feed chamber.

Step Eight Prime and paint for exterior use to your taste. Cut the wire into four 15" lengths. Bend these in half, then insert into small whisker holes drilled into the face.

Step Nine Hack saw the head off the 16d nail after hammering it halfway into the post.

Window Box

If you've ever wished that birds would come right to your window to feed, now you can sneak a peek through the tulips. Refill the feed simply by raising your window and opening the flower bed lid.

Materials List

	1 x 11-1/4" x 14" Pine
	1 x 7-1/2" x 21-5/8" Pine
	1 x 6-3/4" x 21-5/8" Pine
	1 x 5" x 23-1/2" Pine
2	1 x 4" x 8-1/2" Pine
2	1 x 7/8" x 7-3/8" Pine
	1 x 7/8" x 14" Pine
2	1/4" x 1-1/2" x 24" Lath
2	1/4" x 1-1/2" x 5-3/8" Lath
9	1 x 4" x 4-1/2" Pine
9	5/16" x 4-1/4"–7-1/4" Dowels
2	2-1/2" Hinges
	Glue and assorted nails

Step One Mark a point 3-13/16" from each end of the 6-3/4" x 21-5/8" side piece on the long bottom edge. Draw and cut a line from each of these points to the upper corners. Cut a long notch 1/2" x 10-1/2" centered into the bottom edge, or cut 2 or 3 notches (as in the photo). Lay this piece on top of the 7-1/2" x 21-5/8" side piece, trace the diagonal edges to the bottom corners, then 3/4" lines perpendicular to the bottom edge. Cut along these lines. Cut a 60° bevel on one short edge of each 4" x 8-1/2" side piece.

Step Two Glue and nail the notched side to the two 4" sides, with the bottom (notched) edge flush with the 4" beveled edges. Join the other big side opposite to form the window box, then join it to one long edge of the 11-1/4" x 14" tray base.

Step Three Lay the 5" x 23-1/2" lid on top and mark the screw holes and outline of the hinges. Chisel the hinge area out of the lid edge to recess them flush. Clip 1/8" off each corner for drainage. Install the lid with hinges.

Step Four Miter the corner edges of all the lath, then glue and tack them around the lid edge flush with the bottom. Miter the four edges of the 1 x 7/8" strips where they join, then glue and nail them to the tray edge.

Step Five Cut each flower and leaf piece from one of the 4" x 4-1/2" block. Drill 5/16" holes into the lid, the flower bottoms and through the leaf centers. Join them with glue. Paint to your taste.

Step Six This feeder can be attached with steel brackets on top of your window sill (as shown), or lower so that the flower bed is flush with the sill.

Breakfast Tray

Start their day off right with a bountiful banquet. This feeder is easy to stock, delightful to watch, and a real treat for almost any of the bird persuasion. What mother wouldn't drop her worm in favor of this early bird special.

Materials List

> 3/4" x 17" x 23" *Plywood*
> 2 1/4" x 1-1/2" x 24-1/4" *Lath*
> 2 1/4" x 1-1/2" x 18" *Lath*
> 2 1 x 12 x 14" *Pine*
> 2 1 x 3" x 14" *Pine*
> 1 x 4-7/8" x 11-1/2" *Pine*
> 2 1" *Hinges*
> 4 #10 *Wood screws*
> *Vase*
> *Cup and saucer*
> *Bowl*
> *Flatware*
> *Glue and assorted nails*
> *Epoxy*

Step One The only component you must build is the cereal box, but you may prefer to make this oversize tray rather than incorporate a ready-made cafeteria tray. Bevel each edge of the 3/4" plywood at 45°. Cut the bottom corners off each lath strip at 45°. These will butt against each other at each tray corner. Glue and tack the lath to the tray bevels. Drill a 3/16" hole at each corner for drainage. Prime and paint for exterior use.

Step Two Cut a 5/8" x 6" slot centered in the bottom edge of one of the 12 x 14" box panels. Glue and nail the 1 x 12's to the 1 x 3" panels to form the box. Let dry, then sand the seams. Prime and paint the box and lid, decorating it as you wish. Epoxy the box to the tray, then reinforce with #10 screws from the underside into the box corners. Install the lid using the two hinges.

Step Three All the other table items should be fastened in place with epoxy. For periodic cleaning, use a whisk broom or you can even hose it down.

Country Storefronts

This replica of quaint village shops might appeal more to you than window shopping birds, but the goods spilling onto the sidewalk are sure to get their attention. Stock each bin with different feeds, and see which birds stop by on their way through town.

Country Storefronts

Materials List

	1 x 12 x 24-1/2" Pine
	1 x 10" x 24-1/2" Pine
4	*1 x 6-3/4" x 12-3/4" Pine*
	1 x 7" x 24-1/2" Pine
	1 x 2-5/8" x 24-1/2" Pine
	1 x 4-5/8" x 26" Pine
	1 x 7-1/16" x 9" Pine (optional)
4	*5/8" x 6-1/4" Dowels*
	1/4" x 1" x 25" Lath
2	*1/4" x 1" x 11-3/8" Lath*
	1/4" x 15" x 24-1/2" Plywood
	13-1/4" x 24-1/2" Plexiglass
	1/8" Scrap plywood (optional)
	24-1/2" Continuous hinge
	Cabinet knob
	Glue and assorted nails

Step One Rip cut a 60° bevel along one long edge of the 10" x 24-1/2" piece. To cut the peak in the side and interior walls, the pitch is 30° and centered 4-3/4" from one edge. Cut the 2-5/8" x 24-1/2" strip with 60° bevels on both long edges.

Step Two With glue and nails, join the back and four parallel walls onto the 12 x 24-1/2" base, securing them with the narrow top strip across the shorter roof slope. If you wish to add the optional slanted floor baffles, bevel cut the short edges at 45°, then glue and nail them into place.

Step Three Cut the roofline and all windows and doors out of the 1/4" plywood sheet. Cut and attach optional trim pieces cut from 1/8" scrap plywood. Paint this panel. Lay the plexiglass sheet beneath this panel, cut semi-circles inside the doorways, then put both in place over the front of the walls. Pre-drill, glue and nail into place.

Step Four Cut 60° bevels on both long edges of the 7" x 24-1/2" roof panel. Secure this to the other roof strip with the long hinge. Install the knob near the bottom edge center.

Step Five Cut 60° parallel bevels along both long edges of the 4-5/8" x 26" awning panel. Cut the tops of the four dowel support post with a 30° bevel. Glue and nail these pieces into place. Signs cut from 1/8" scrap can be hung with small eyescrews. Tack the lath lip into place, then paint the rest of the assembly.

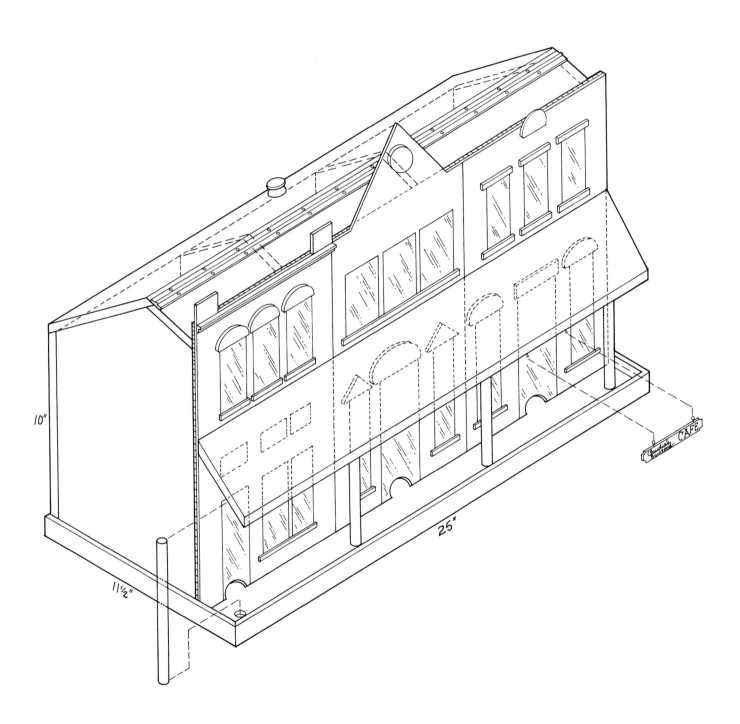

10"

11½"

25"

CAFE

Flying Aces Hangar

After a tough day of aerial acrobatics, your plumed pilots will be happy to taxi down this runway for a snack. A hinged loading door in the rear lets you keep this feeder well stocked.

Materials List

	1 x 12 x 24" Pine
2	1 x 6 x 12" Pine
2	1 x 8-1/8" x 9-1/4" Pine
	1/2" x 12" 1/4-round Molding
	12-1/2" x 14-3/4" Aluminum sheeting
2	3" x 4" Aluminum sheeting
2	1" Hinges
	Cabinet knob
	1/4" x 1" x 4" Lath
	1/4" x 5/8" x 5" Lath
	1/4" x 1" x 6-1/2" Lath
	1/4" x 8-1/2" Dowel
	3-1/2" Heavy wire
	3" x 3-1/2" Stiff cloth
	Toy airplane
	Glue and assorted nails

Step One Cut a 4-1/2" x 5-3/4" front doorway out of one of the 8-1/8" x 9-1/4" wall pieces. Save the cut-out. Draw a line 7/8" above the top doorway edge and parallel to it. Everything above this line will be the arc area. Trace the arc neatly, lay this piece over the other same size piece, then cut the arc in both. Cut a 3-1/2" x 5" hole, centered 4-1/2" up from the bottom edge, in this second wall.

Step Two Glue and nail these arc-top walls to the 6 x 12" side walls, butting the side pieces inside the end pieces. Glue and nail the two 1/4-round strips to the top edges of the side walls, rounded faces out and flush with the arc. Let dry. Glue and nail this assembly to one end of the 24" base.

Step Three Cut a 3-3/8" x 4-15/16" rectangle from the front door cut-out. Round the top inner edge for clearance. Cut a fan shape out of each 3" x 4" piece of aluminum. Tack a straight edge of each fan to the opposite side edges of the door panel, flush with the outer door surface. Glue and tack the 4" lath strip to the inside top of the door opening to act as a door-jamb. Install the knob, then hinge the door in place.

Step Four Tack the aluminum roof sheet into place. If you want extra strength, cut and bend a section of stove pipe instead, and pre-drill the nail holes. Leaving a 1" stem, bend the 3-1/2" wire into a question mark and close the circle. Sharpen the stem to a point with a file.

Step Five Cut converging tapers on opposite edges of the cloth. Glue or stitch the funnel-shaped wind sock around the wire hoop. Drill a hole 3/4" into one end of the dowel that is 1/32" wider than the wire stem. Whittle and sand this end of the dowel to round it. Drill a 1/4" hole in the base, then glue the dowel in place. Also glue the airplane in place.

Step Six Cut the wings from the 5/8" x 5" lath. Paint them, along with the 1" x 6-1/2" sign. Paint the entire structure to your taste, then glue and tack the wings and sign above the doorway.

Step Seven To avoid drainage problems and soggy feed, you can either mount the structure to slope away from the chamber, or add a 1 x 7-3/4" x 12" raised floor before attaching the chamber to the base.

Intergalactic Snack

To boldly go where no bird feeder has gone before…That is the mission of this stylish seed shuttle. It is a shining tribute to the birds that first inspired man's flight—a spacecraft with real star quality.

Materials List

    1/4" x 16" x 16" Mahogany plywood
    1/4" x 10" x 14-1/2" Mahogany plywood
3 *3/8" x 9" Dowels*
    7/8" x 1" dia. PVC pipe
    Glues

Step One Cut the base plate from the 16" square plywood, following the diagram. All edges are cut at 90°. Save the scrap.

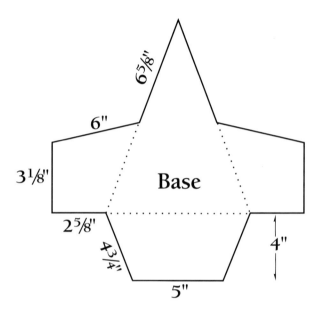

Step Two Cut the two sides of the fuselage from the 10" x 14-1/2" plywood with a 42° diagonal cut. Trim these into isosceles triangles with 90° cuts. Bevel the third sides at 48°. Then go back and cut another 3/32" at 42° halfway down each long edge to open up a slot for the top fin.

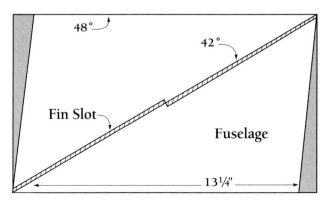

94

Step Three Cut a kite-shaped top fin from plywood scrap. Then cut a 6-1/8" x 4-5/8" x 4-5/8" triangle from scrap. (The dotted line shows the glue seam with the fuselage.) All edges are cut at 90°.

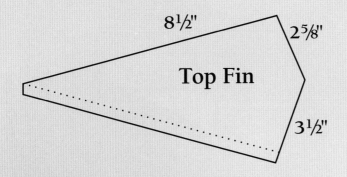

8½"

2⅝"

Top Fin

3½"

Step Four Run a good bead of glue along every edge to be joined as you assemble the fuselage to the base. Weights can be leaned against the sides and rubber bands clamped around the nose. Let dry, then glue the top fin into the slot, and the triangular baffle into the fuselage.

Step Five Cut three 5/8" x 5" strips from plywood scrap. Miter them and glue them to the rear of the base to form a lip for the feed tray.

Step Six Cut the PVC in half lengthwise to form two radar dishes. Drill a 3/8" hole in each one. Sharpen the ends of the dowels in a pencil sharpener. Glue the radar dishes onto two of the dowels. Glue the dowels in place with silicone sealant. Caulk all the other seams with silicone after the dowels have dried. Prime and paint for exterior use. This feeder can be hung or post mounted.

Lighthouse Lunchbox

If you're a coastal dweller, this feeder could be the perfect yard ornament. You may even wish to install a working beacon which will draw extra insect snacks for night birds.

Materials List

	1 x 6-1/2" x 21" Pine
2	3/8" x 3-1/2" x 21" Cedar or redwood
2	3/8" x 3" x 10" Cedar or redwood
	1 x 4" x 14-1/2" Pine
2	1/4" x 3" x 14-1/2" Plywood
2	3-1/2" x 10" Plexiglass panels
	3" x 19" PVC pipe
	4" x 4" x 4" Pine block
3	1/4" x 2-1/2" Dowels
	Scrap plastic packaging or bottle caps
	Scrap of window screen
	Shingles
	Glue and assorted nails
4	#10 Wood screws

Step One Bevel cut both long edges of the 6-1/2" x 21" pine base at 45°. Glue and nail both 3-1/2" x 21" side panels to these beveled edges. Sand both short ends flush, then glue and nail the end panels onto these ends. Trim and sand excess flush with sides after the glue has dried. This tray will hold excess feed, but could also be a wider base with a lath lip.

Step Two Cut two 5" blocks from the 1 x 4" pine. Cut two roof-peak tapers at the top of each block. Cut three tapered braces, each 3-1/2" long parallel to the grain, from the remaining 1 x 4" to match the roof-peak angles. Glue and nail the two 1/4" plywood roof panels onto these three braces, spacing them (as shown in the photo) so as to fit either side of the two upright blocks.

Step Three You can mill your own shingles from 1/8" stock, or purchase doll house shingles. Apply successive beads of silicone across both roof panels, and apply each layer of shingles, staggering them, from the bottom up.

Step Four Cut two 3/8" grooves into each of the upright blocks, stopping 3/4" short of the bottom edge. These will hold the plexiglass. Bevel cut and chisel an indentation on the outside of one block to accommodate the 3" PVC shape. Using a hole saw, cut a 1-1/2" hole through this block and into the PVC while they are standing together. Glue and bolt them together. Cut three 1" holes spiralling up the cylinder for feeding stations. Cut a 1/4" hole 1" below each of these.

Step Five Glue the cylinder assembly 3" from one end of the tray, reinforcing with two wood screws up from the bottom and into the block. Attach the other block the same way, inserting the plexiglass in place to determine spacing. Remove the plexiglass, drill two 3/8" drainage holes between the blocks, and glue circles of screen over them. (The photo shows dowel pegs for roof alignment, but these are optional.) Cut a rounded notch in the roof to fit around the cylinder.

Step Six This beacon was lathe-turned from a 4" block of wood. Another effective approach would be to join concentric circles of wood with a cross-cut section of a plastic bottle in the middle. The bottom must fit neatly inside the cylinder to act as a stopper.

Step Seven After painting the structure, the dowel perches can be glued into place. Sections of curved plastic packaging can be glued under the feeding holes with silicone or epoxy. If you prefer, glue bottle caps into these holes and pack suet into them for the winter months.

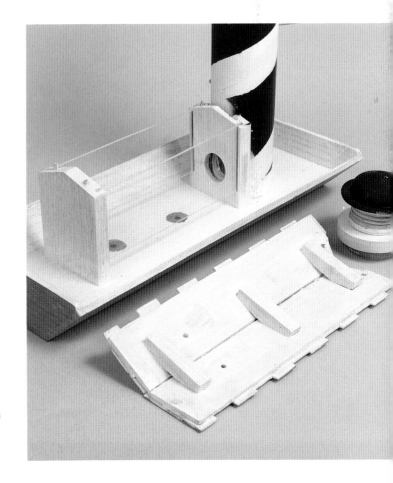

Tropical Island

Birds can snack after bathing in this tropical paradise. Pipe in a little reggae or calypso music, and they may never want to leave.

Materials List

	1 x 12 x 14" Pine
	1 x 8-1/2" x 10-1/2" Pine
2	1/2" x 13" Copper pipe
6	1" Styrofoam balls
6	Paper clips
	Aluminum sheeting scraps
2	#9 Wood screws
	Clear silicone sealant

Step One Cut an irregular oval out of each pine piece using a coping, jig or band saw. Using a router, sander or hand tools, round off the top edges of these pieces if you want a naturally tapered beach and greenery. Cut a 5" circle out of the center of the smaller piece to cradle the feed. Using a bead of silicone and woodscrews from the underside, join these two pieces.

Step Two Bend each copper pipe gently into curved palm trunks. Use tin snips to cut palm fronds out of aluminum sheeting. Leave 3/8" x 1" stems that will be glued into the pipes with silicone. Straighten one end of each paper clip. Insert these straight ends through the styrofoam balls until the looped end is flush. These wire stems will be inserted with the frond stems. Paint the trunks, fronds and coconuts with enamel before gluing them into place with silicone.

Step Three Drill two 1/2" holes slanted into the island base. Silicone the trees into place and let dry. Paint the island well with enamel to seal it against the rotting effect of water. You can either float the island or rest it on a brick inside your bird bath.

Seed for Sail

You'll have more than gulls circling this vessel of victuals, eager to sample the catch of the day. Hang a few mesh bags full of thistle seed over the sides, fill the hold with tasty morsels, then run signal flags up the mast that say "good eats."

Materials List

	1 x 4" x 24" Pine
	1 x 2-5/8" x 3-3/4" Pine
	1/4" x 1" x 7" Pine
	1 x 2" x 4" Pine
6	1/8" x 1-3/4" x 25"–28-1/2" Poplar
	1/4" Lath scrap
	1/2" x 36" Dowel
	1/4" x 17" Dowel
2	1/4" x 13" Dowels
	1/4" x 11" Dowel
	1/4" x 7" Dowel
5	1/4" x 3-3/4" Dowels
4	Eyescrews
	Nylon string
	7" x 13" Canvas
	Toy bucket, anchor and chain
3	1" dia. Screens
	Glue and assorted nails

Step One Cut the curved hull bottom with an 80° bevel all around. Cut the stern block as shown in the diagram. The 2-7/8" bottom edge should be cut on an 80° bevel. Glue the stern block on top of the hull bottom. Let dry.

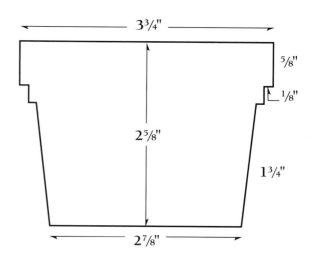

Step Two Each end of the 7" bow stem should be cut at parallel 45° angles. Cut one end of two 1-3/4" x 25" strips at 45°, then bevel the insides of these edges slightly to join with the bow stem. Run a good bead of glue on the lower stern, hull bottom edges and lower bow stem. Tack the side strips to the stern, then clamp them to the bow stem, which gets glued to the hull bottom. Let dry.

Step Three Sand the bow joint down to a taper before attaching the next side strips. Glue, tack, clamp, and let it dry. Sand the new bow joint before attaching the last strips. After they have dried, sand the bow and trim the top edges flush with the stern block.

Step Four Glue the 2" x 4" block, centered 15" from the stern, to the hull bottom. Glue a brace cut from 1/4" scrap over this, resting across the middle side strips. Enclose the bow with two triangular pieces of scrap if you wish.

Step Five Drill a 1/2" hole through the center brace and into the block to support the mast. Drill three 1/4" drain holes across the bottom, then glue the screens over top. Drill a 1/4" hole into the bow stem to support the 7" bow sprit. Drill a 1/4" hole at each corner of the stern and both sides of the center brace to support the 3-3/4" posts for the tarp. Glue all these dowels into place.

Step Six Drill a 1/4" hole through the mast, 7-1/2" up, for the 17" boom. Drill a 1/4" hole 3" from the mast top for the 3-3/4" yardarm, and another 9-1/2" from the top for the 11" yardarm. Glue these dowels into place. Install an eyescrew next to each tarp support post, then rig the boat with nylon string.

Step Seven Glue each long edge of the canvas around a 13" dowel. Let dry, then drape it over the boom. The dowels can either be tied or glued directly onto the tarp posts. Mount this feeder on a post.

Victorian Gazebo

Nothing quite matches the charm of turn-of-the-century architecture. This feeder could serve as an attractive focal point in a formal garden, at the same time luring colorful creatures to feed.

Materials List

	1 x 11-1/4" x 11-1/4" Pine
	1 x 10" x 10" Pine
4	*9" Triangles of 1/2" plywood*
	1/4" x 4-1/2" Dowel
	3/8" x 8" Dowel
	1/8" x 5-1/2" Dowel
10	*5/8" Wooden beads*
4	*3/4" x 3/4" x 5-1/2" Pine posts*
4	*3/4" x 1-1/16" x 1-1/16" Pine blocks*
4	*1/2" x 3/4" x 8" Pine*
4	*1/4 x 1-1/2" x 11-5/8" Lath*
3	*1/4 x 3/4" x 8-1/2" Lath rails*
18	*1/4 x 1/4" x 3" Lath ballisters*
8	*1/4 x 3/4" x 2-3/4" Lath scrolls*
	Doll house shingles
	Aluminum sheet scrap
	Clear silicone and assorted nails

Step One Cut and sand the two foundation plates from 1 x 12 pine. Cut a 5" circle out of the center of the smaller plate using a jigsaw, and sand.

Step Two Rip cut (from 1 x stock) the four 5-1/2" square posts, then cross-cut each post into a 3" and a 2-1/2" length. Next, rip cut the four 1/2" strips (from 1 x), each measuring 8" long. These will be butt joined to form the top frame that supports the roof. Finally, rip a 5" length of 1 x into a 1-1/16" width, then cut four 1-1/16" blocks to go on top of the posts.

Step Three Miter cut four 11-5/8" lengths of lath to form the lip around the base. Next, rip cut three 8-1/2" lengths of lath to a width of 3/4" for the rails. Miter cut all but the two ends which will join the posts at the opening of the feeder. Out of a 13" length of the same lath, rip four 1/4" strips, then a fifth strip from what would have been the fourth 3/4" x 8-1/2" rail. Cut these into eighteen 3" ballisters.

Step Four Measure and glue the four 3" sections of corner posts into place, then glue the three rails around the top. Let dry, then wedge and glue the ballisters into place. Let dry. Reinforce the corner posts with a nail or screw from underneath. Then glue and top nail this assembly onto the bottom plate with the two grains running perpendicular. Glue and nail the mitered lath lip around the perimeter. A small drainage hole can be drilled in each corner.

Step Five Glue the 1-1/16" blocks onto the 2-1/2" upper post sections. Glue and nail the roof frame together with butt joints. Let dry. Drill 3/8" holes, each 1/2" deep, into the centers of the upper and lower post sections. Cut the 3/8" dowel into four 2" lengths, thread two wooden beads over each one, and join all the post sections with glue. While the glue is wet, align the roof frame over the posts and glue it in place onto the post blocks.

Step Six Two of the three sides of each 9" roof triangle can be bevel cut for tighter joinery. Lean these roof panels together, joining them with silicone. Let dry, then glue onto the roof frame.

Step Seven Sharpen one end of the 1/4" dowel to a point. Drill perpendicular 1/8" holes through the center of this dowel, then insert two 2-3/4" lengths of 1/8" dowel through the holes. Glue in place. Cut the letters N, E, W and S from

aluminum sheet, and silicone them onto the ends of these small dowels. Glue two beads, pre-drilled with 1/4" holes, onto the main dowel either side of these small dowels.

Step Eight Using a coping or band saw, cut the eight scroll pieces from lath. They can be glued into place after they are painted. Drill a 1/4" hole at the apex of the roof. Glue the weather-vane assembly into this hole.

Step Nine Apply successive beads of silicone onto two opposite roof panels, and apply each row of shingles from the bottom tier up. Let dry, then trim the diagonal edges with a coping saw from the bottom up. Apply shingles to the other two roof panels, let dry, and trim. Paint the entire piece to your taste. Apply two coats of polyurethane to the roof shingles.

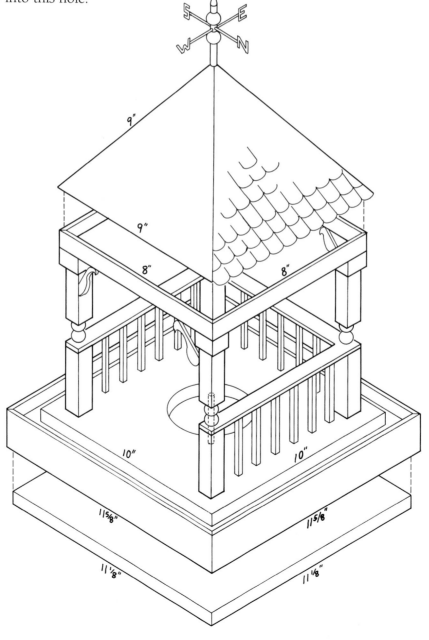

Castle Keep

This aviary compound features all the amenities: house, rooftop bath and turret feeders, proving that a bird's home is his castle. Fortify your feathered friends in this medieval marvel.

Materials List

4	1 x 12 x 10" Pine
2	1 x 8-3/8" x 8-3/8" Pine
4	1 x 5" x 20" Pine
4	1/4 x 1-1/2" x 20-1/2" Lath
4	2" x 12" PVC pipe
	7-3/8" x 7-3/8" Plastic tray
8	1/2" x 1/2" x 8-3/8" Pine
4	1 x 3-1/2" Circles of pine
33	3/4" x 3/4" x 1-1/4" Pine blocks
	3-1/4" x 4-3/4" Pine door
4	1/4" x 6-1/4" Dowels
	Aluminum sheet scrap
4	Small eyescrews
	9" Chain
	3-1/2" x 4-1/4" Wire mesh
	Glue and assorted finishing nails

Step One It should be noted that, depending on the dimensions of the rooftop tray (or baking pan) you find, the size of the castle can be adapted accordingly. So find your bird bath tray first.

Step Two Miter cut the 1 x 12 pine to 10" lengths (or to fit other tray) to form the castle walls. Cut square notches in the top edges for battlements. Rip cut eight 8-3/8" pine strips 1/2" square. Miter cut these to recess into the top and bottom of the castle walls. Glue and nail

the bottom tier of these, recessed 3/4" from the bottom edge of each wall.

Step Three Glue and nail the four wall sections together. Cut the two 8-3/8" square panels from 1 x pine. Glue and nail one of these, recessed 1/2" from the top of the battlement cutouts. Glue and nail the remaining mitered 1/2" square strips above this panel into place.

Step Four Cut the 2" PVC pipe into 12" lengths. Cut a 1/2" x 1-1/2" slot in one end of each pipe. Pre-drill and screw, at top and bottom, each pipe to the walls at the front and back corners.

Step Five Cut four mitered 5" x 20" planks from 1 x pine to form the blue moat. Glue and nail, from the inside bottom edge of the castle walls, these moat planks into place. Glue and tack the lath lip into place around the perimeter. Finally, insert the 8-3/8" square bottom panel into place, and secure with glue and angled nails.

Step Six Cut four 5-pointed asterisk shapes from the 3-1/2" circles of 1 x pine. Also cut four 1-1/2" circles of pine. Rip cut 3/4" strips of 1 x pine, to be cut into 33 blocks of 1-1/4" lengths. Glue five of these onto the tops of each asterisk. Glue and screw the 1-1/2" circles beneath them. Drill 1/4" holes into the top centers to accommodate the dowel flagstaffs.

Step Seven Cut the four lengths of 1/4" dowel. Notch one end with a fine coping saw blade. Cut long triangles of aluminum sheet to wedge into place as flags. Glue these flags into place.

Step Eight Cut a 3-1/4" x 4-3/4" door from 1 x pine. Round off one end. Glue and nail into place. Glue the remaining nine blocks into place around the doorway. After these are

painted, the wire mesh and eyescrews with chain will be installed. Drill the bird house entry hole above the door.

Step Nine Paint as you wish. The mortar lines can be added with a small-tipped paint pencil. The turret tops are removable in order to load seed into the turret towers. Drainage holes can be added to the moat.

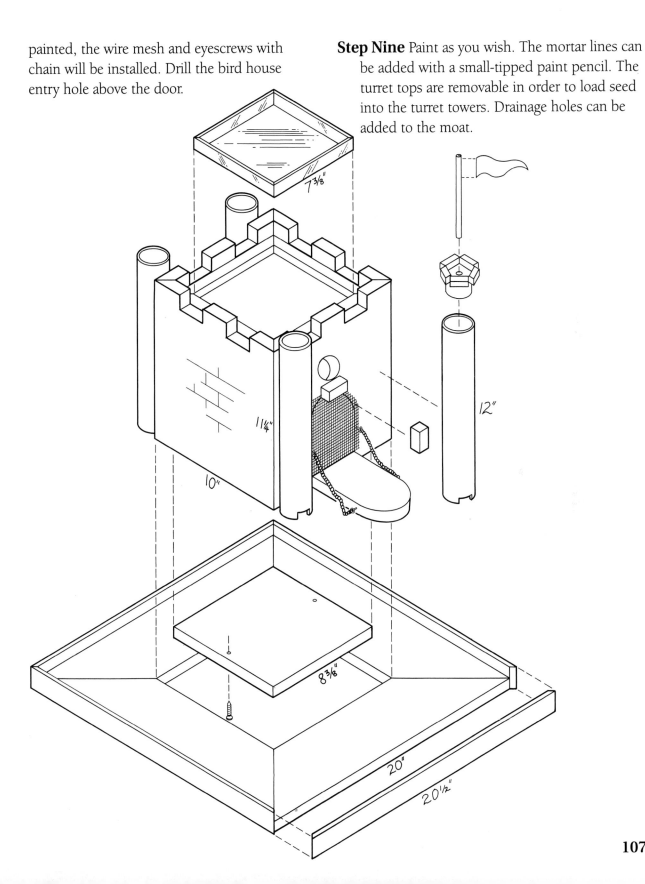

Carousel Cuisine

Fanciful animals orbiting a seed dispenser—how could a hungry bird resist? And what if the saddled species were all sorts of birds? Then again, you may elect to display this spectacular feeder indoors with nuts and candies for our own kind.

Materials List

2 *1/2" x 16" x 16" Mahogany plywood*
8 *1/2" x 7" Dowels*
  1/2" x 13" Dowel
8 *3/16" x 7" Dowels*
  3/16" x 2" Dowel
8 *1/4" x 6-5/8" x 9-1/2" x 9-1/2" Plywood triangles*
8 *1/4" x 1-3/8" x 6-3/4" Mahogany plywood*
8 *1/4" x 3/8" x 6-15/16" Mahogany plywood*
8 *1/4" x 3-1/2" x 3-3/4" Mahogany plywood*
8 *4" x 5-1/4" Medium acrylic safety glazing*
8 *1/2" x 1/2" x 6-3/8" Molding*
  1-1/4" Wooden bead
  3/8" Wooden bead
  Toothpicks
  Glue

Step One Cut two identical equilateral octagons from the 16" square plywood. Draw the four intersecting lines from each pair of opposing points on both pieces. Mark 4-3/8" in from each of these points along all eight spokes to determine the centers of the support posts. On one piece, draw four more intersecting lines between the midpoints of each edge. Mark 3" in from each edge along these bisecting spokes to determine the animal mounting posts.

Step Two Line up both hexagons, the piece with more lines drawn on top of the other. Drill 1/2" holes through both pieces on the centers marked for support posts. Drill 3/16" holes on the centers marked for animal mounting posts. Drill a 1/2" hole in the very center of one of the hexagons. With a compass, mark a 6" circle in the center of the other hexagon and cut it out with a jigsaw.

Step Three Each of the eight support posts must be rip cut with two 1/8" grooves 135° apart. See the diagram to make a jig that will facilitate these two cuts. Fill the lower ends of these grooves with 1-1/4" lengths of toothpicks, glued flush with the bottoms to act as stops for the acrylic panes.

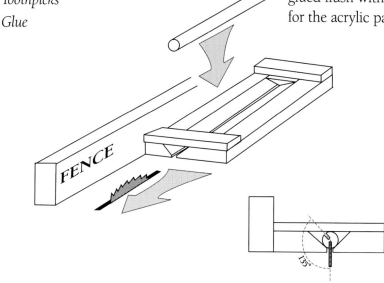

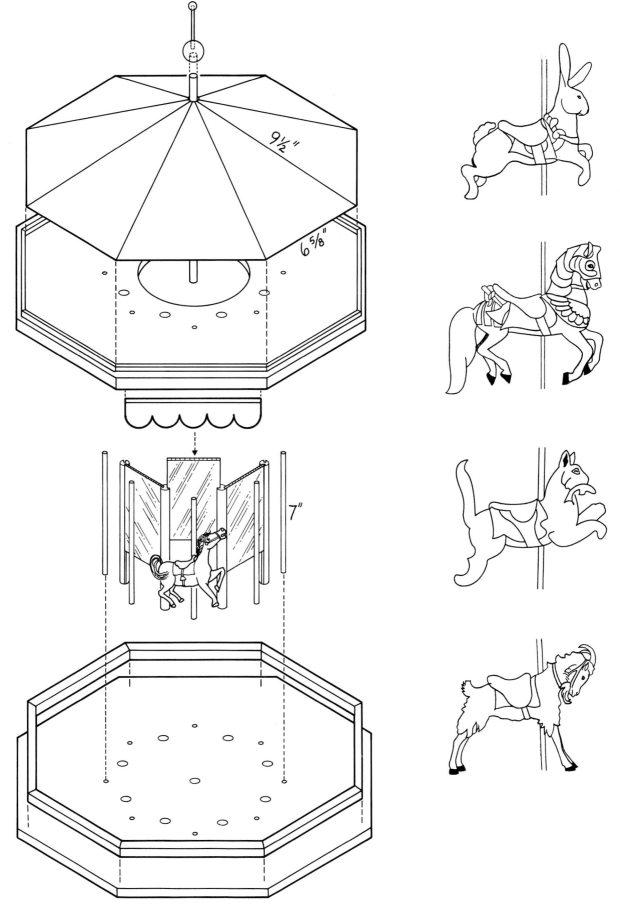

9½"

6 5/8"

7"

Step Four The lip on the lower hexagon can be made with 1/2" stock—square or rounded, half-round or other mouldings. Miter cut the ends at 67-1/2°, then glue them around the perimeter. Cut five rounded scallops into one edge of each 1-3/8" x 6-3/4" piece. Miter cut the ends to 67-1/2° and glue around the outer edge of the other hexagon. (Glue the top edges flush if you plan to install outdoors, since drainage will be a factor.) Miter the 3/8" strips the same way, and glue on as trim.

Step Five Paint all dowels and both hexagons, except the 1/2" ends of dowels to be glued, before joining. The acrylic panes can be cut using an inexpensive plastics cutting tool with a straight edge. Glue and tap each dowel into the bottom hexagon. Insert the acrylic panes as you go so as to align the support posts before they dry. You must also insert all dowels into the upper hexagon and tap into place before the glue dries. Let everything dry.

Step Six Miter cut one long edge of each roof triangle at 70°. Lay the panels together over tape strips, edge to edge, bevels up. Run a good bead of glue down each seam, fold the panels into a cone and tape the last seam. Let dry, inverted. Drill a 1/2" hole at the apex from the underside. Glue the 1/2" center post into the base. Check the fit of the roof over this post, then trim if necessary and sand all edges and seams.

Step Seven Drill a 1/2" hole 3/4 of the way into the larger wooden bead. Drill a 3/16" hole in the top, and into the smaller bead. Glue this assembly together, then onto the apex of the roof. Paint the roof and spire. Pennant may be glued to the spire's shaft.

Step Eight Using the patterns, or your own imagination, cut the animals out of 1/4" plywood with a coping or band saw. Paint them as you wish, and glue them to the posts.

Baths

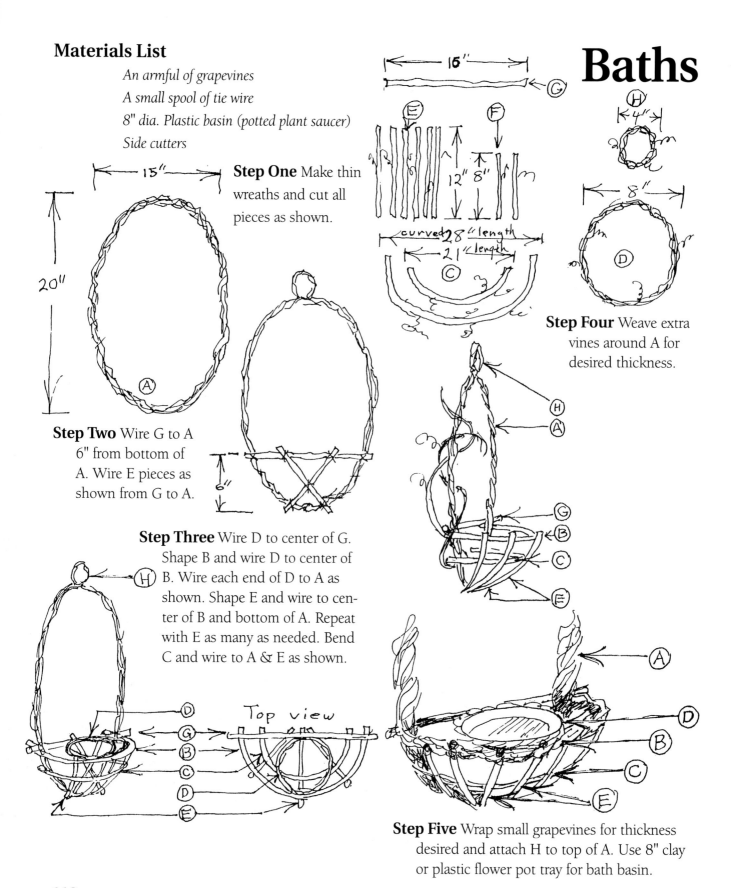

Materials List

An armful of grapevines
A small spool of tie wire
8" dia. Plastic basin (potted plant saucer)
Side cutters

Step One Make thin wreaths and cut all pieces as shown.

Step Two Wire G to A 6" from bottom of A. Wire E pieces as shown from G to A.

Step Three Wire D to center of G. Shape B and wire D to center of B. Wire each end of D to A as shown. Shape E and wire to center of B and bottom of A. Repeat with E as many as needed. Bend C and wire to A & E as shown.

Step Four Weave extra vines around A for desired thickness.

Step Five Wrap small grapevines for thickness desired and attach H to top of A. Use 8" clay or plastic flower pot tray for bath basin.

112

Wall Hanging Bath

Not all bird baths sit on pedestals.
This woven basket cradles a basin and
belongs on a vine-covered wall next to a
garden. It could also be used as a feeder.

Swimming Pool

Even birds need a recreational splash now and then. And what fun you'll have watching them do back flips and belly flops off the high dive. Sprinkle some seed around the patio furniture, and watch them frolic.

Materials List

	1/2" x 12" x 24" Plywood
	3/4" or 1" x 12" x 24" Plywood
2	1/4" x 1-1/2" x 24-1/2" Lath
2	1/4" x 1-1/2" x 12-1/2" Lath
	1/4" x 1-1/2" x 6" Lath
	3/4" x 3/4" x 1-3/8" Pine
	3/32" x 46" Brass rod
	1/16" x 40" Brass wire
	3-3/4" dia. Dome from plastic bottle
	3/4" x 1" dia. Dowel
	5/16" Wooden bead
2	7/8" x 3-1/4" Grosgrain ribbon
	Polyurethane (can be water base)
7	#9 Wood screws
	Glue and brads

Step One Use a jigsaw to cut a kidney-shaped hole through the 3/4" plywood to form the pool basin. Then, using a coping saw, cut a taper into each side of the 1-3/8" pine block to form the pedestal for the table. Glue the sanded pedestal onto the deck, reinforcing it with a wood screw from underneath. Glue the deck onto the 1/2" plywood base, reinforcing it with the six remaining screws from underneath.

Step Two Miter the edges of the four long lath strips to fit around the base and deck. Glue

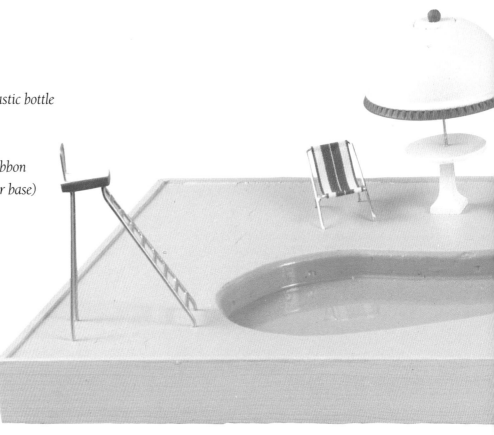

and tack the lath around the edges. Cut the 6" lath piece into the following: (2) 5/8" x 3-1/2" diving boards, 3/4" x 1-1/16" lifeguard seat, 5/8" x 5/8" step, and a 1-1/2" dia. circle. Drill a 3/32" hole through the center of this circle, another into the pedestal, another through the 3/4" section of dowel, and another into the wooden bead. Glue the dowel into the top of the dome. Let dry. Using glue in all joints and seams, assemble the patio table with a 4" length of brass rod.

Step Three All the furniture is soldered together using brass rod for the ladders and vertical supports, with brass wire for the chairs, hand rails, and seat back. They are painted silver after assembly. The high dive and lifeguard chair stand 3-1/8" tall. The low dive is 3/8" above the deck. The chair back frames are 2-1/2" long and 1-1/8" wide. The chair seat frames are 2" long. Each piece of furniture is glued into 3/8" deep holes in the deck. The ribbon is glued or sewn to the chair frames. After painting everything, coat the basin with 2–3 coats of polyurethane.

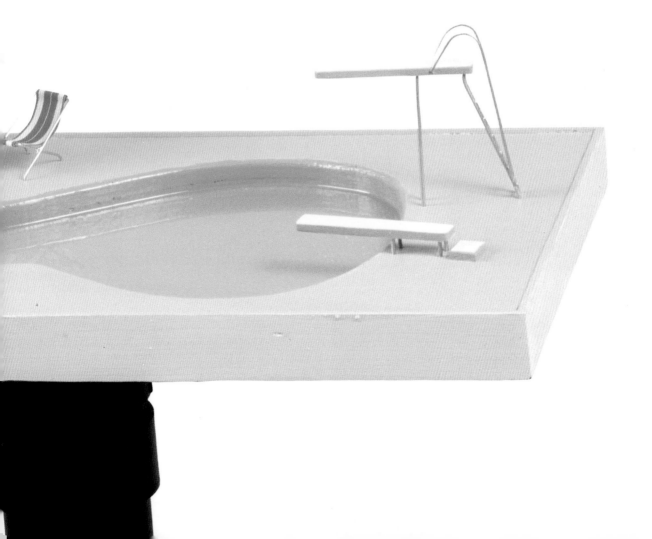

Drive-Thru Bird Wash

Falcons and Thunderbirds have been zipping through these automated tunnels of suds for years now, emerging clean and glistening. Isn't it time to offer this dandy device to all the dirty birds in your neighborhood?

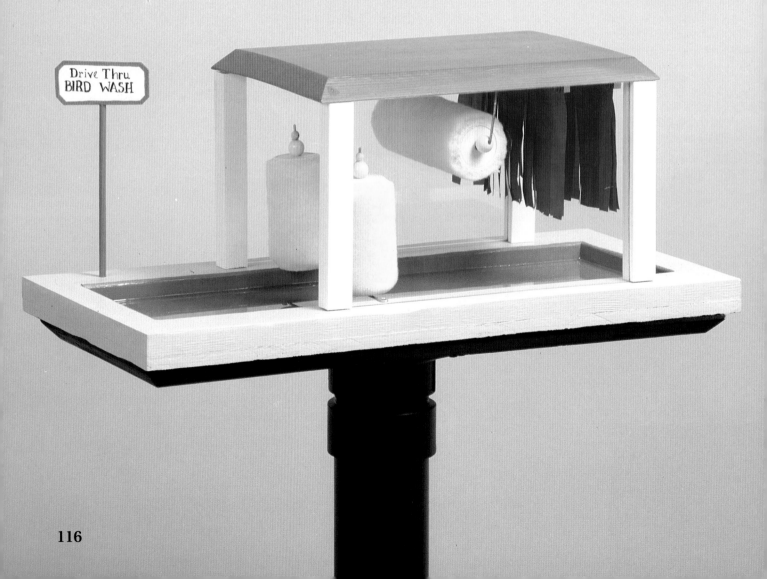

Materials List

1 x 10-7/8" x 24" Pine

1/2" x 10-7/8" x 24" Plywood

1 x 9" x 13-3/4" Pine

4   3/4" x 1" x 7" Pine

2   7" x 11-3/4" Plexiglass

2   1/4" x 3/8" x 7-1/4" Pine

2   4-3/4" x 7-1/4" Rip-stop nylon

6-1/4" Paint roller

2   4" Paint rollers

6   3/4" x 1-15/32" dia. Pine disks

3/32" x 14-1/4" Brass rod

2   3/32" x 7" Brass rods

4   5/8" Wooden balls

2   5/16" Wooden balls

1/4" x 8" Dowel

4   1/4" x 1-3/4" Dowels

1/8" x 1-1/2" x 3-3/8" Lath

8   #8 Wood screws

Glue and assorted nails

Small wire staples

Polyurethane (can be water base)

Step One Cut a 6-1/2" x 21" hole in the center of the 24" pine. Rip cut a 1/4" deep groove down one 3/4" face of each 7" pine post to accept the plexiglass. Cut a 45° bevel on all four edges of the pine roof block.

Step Two Drill a 3/32" hole through the center of each pine disk. If you can't find a dowel that fits snugly into the paint roller, cut the disks from 1 x stock with a hole saw. Glue the disks into the rollers flush with the ends.

Step Three Bend the 14-1/4" rod into a tall C-shaped rectangle, the long back of which will be tacked to the ceiling with staples. The long side measures 7-1/4". The bracket bends 90° down to 2-1/4", leaving 1-1/4" on each end to

bend 90° through the wooden bead and into the disk. Bend both shorter rods into L-shapes, the long stem of which measures 5-1/4". Bend the shorter ends into tight eyelets to accept the mounting screws. Slip the rollers onto the stems, and glue the wooden beads on top.

Step Four Cut 4" slits into the nylon to make fringe. Tack these strips to the 1/4" x 3/8" x 7-1/4" pine, then glue and tack them to the ceiling 1-1/4" and 3-1/2" from one edge. Tack staples over the roller support rod 6-1/2" from the same edge. Screw the two upright rollers 3/8" from the edges of the basin, and 10" from one end of the 24" pine.

Step Five Drill a 1/4" hole 1" into the center of one end of each 7" pine post. Drill four 1/4" holes through the 24" pine that form a 8-3/16" x 12-3/8" rectangle. The holes closest to the rollers should be 2-1/8" away from the roller mounting screws.

Step Six Glue a 1-3/4" dowel into each post. Fit the plexiglass into the post grooves, then glue the posts to the base, tapping the dowels into place. Glue and top nail the roof on to the posts. Let dry.

Step Seven Glue the 24" pine base to the 1/2" plywood foundation, reinforcing with the six remaining screws from underneath. Flatten one side of the top inch of the 8" dowel, then glue it to the lath sign. Drill a 1/4" hole in the base, and glue the sign in place.

Step Eight You may want to paint as you assemble, or paint everything after assembly. After painting, apply 2–3 coats of polyurethane to the basin.

Acorn Gourd House

Gourds make wonderful bird houses. Different ways of cultivating various species add to the design possibilities. Hang this giant acorn from your tallest oak.

Materials List

Dipper gourd
Bottle gourd

Step One Select a medium-sized dipper gourd with a tapered bottom for the chamber. Cut off the neck of the gourd at a point just above the largest part of the ball, and clean out the seeds. Save the stem to use for the perch.

Step Two Drill an entrance hole about 1-1/4" dia., or start with a sampler hole and enlarge it using sandpaper wrapped around a pencil. Drill a smaller hole just big enough to accept a piece of the gourd stem for a perch.

Step Three Select a bottle gourd of the same size but with a flatter bottom for the acorn's cap. Cut this gourd just below the widest point. Use the bottom piece for the cap. Drill a small hole in the center of this part.

Insert the stem as the stem of the acorn.

Step Four Fit the cap over the house section and glue them together. Wood burning or painting the cap to look like a real acorn cap will be effective for a natural look. Wood stains of different hues will also enhance the bird house. When you are satisfied with the look you've achieved, spray with a clear coat of acrylic finish.

Thatched Gourd House

Birds may have to evict the gnomes before setting up housekeeping in this elfin-looking abode. Either way, you'll enjoy hanging this enchanting shelter in your yard.

Materials List

Pear-shaped gourd
Spare gourd
Broom corn
2' Raffia
Glue

Step One Select a medium-sized, pear-shaped gourd that is tapered downward to a flat bottom. Drill a 1-1/4" hole in the side of the gourd for an entrance hole. Carefully clean out the seeds. A piece of coat hanger with a small hook on one end is helpful in the cleaning process. Cut off the stem and use it for a perch, gluing it into a pre-drilled hole.

Step Two If you decide to stain your gourd, do so now. Add a coat of clear acrylic after the stain and glue have dried.

Step Three The roof is made from broom corn stalks cut to about 3"–4". Most craft stores carry broom corn. Three layers, glued progressively higher up the gourd, should be enough. You can use a hot glue gun to attach the rows of broom corn.

Step Four The porch roof is cut from the neck of another gourd and glued on. Since the apex of the roof will look ragged from the tips of the broom corn, a cap should be made from the top of another gourd and glued securely on top.

Step Five The thatch is held in place with a band of some natural material like raffia. Dried flowers would add a nice touch, tucked through the raffia band.

Grapevine Summer House

This decorative birdhouse, with its husky vines and coiled tendrils, offers breezy shelter for nesting birds. It can be hung under a porch roof or eaves to keep out rain. It can also be built around a gourd for use in colder climates.

Materials List

An armful of grapevines
A small spool of tie wire
Side cutters

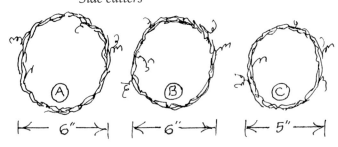

Step One Make thin round wreaths and cut all pieces as shown.

Step Four Attach E to C as shown.

Step Two Start with eight 32" stays and add as many as you desire.

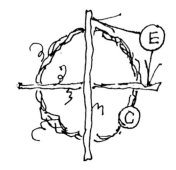

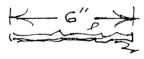

Step Three Start with eight 6" roof vines and add as many as you desire.

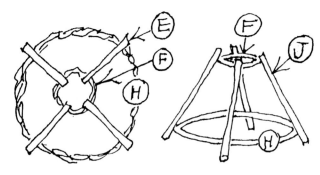

Step Five Attach four rafters as shown, then add more.

Step Six Bend I into tear drop. Attach ends of E 5" from top of tear drop.

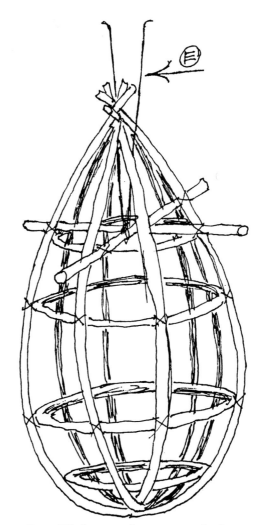

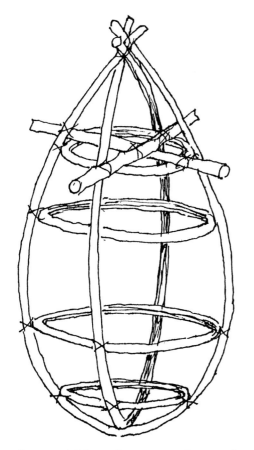

Step Seven Add inside rings as shown, then repeat tear drop stays until walls are as full as you desire.

Step Eight Attach wire to E for later attachment to top ring.

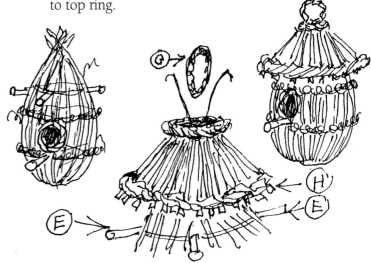

Step Nine Wire door and perch in place, then cut out door. Place roof over hanger wires and wire roof H to E. Tie hanger wires to G. Add small vines to outside for decorative trim.

Thatched Yurt

Asian nomads developed a distinctive round house that was collapsible and featured a domed or conical roof. This design lends itself beautifully to the use of natural materials, and is sure to enhance your outdoor site.

Materials List

	3/8" x 6" dia. Plywood
8	3/8" x 2-1/2" x 5-3/4" Bark-faced pine slats
	1/2" x 18" Green twig, de-barked
	1-1/2" dia. x 20" Bundle of straw
	3/16" x 10' Grapevine
	12' Thin vine or twine
	Tie wire

Step One Drill eight 3/16" holes around the perimeter of the 6" plywood circle, equidistant and 3/8" from the edge. The eight slats can be split off of a pine log to a thickness of 3/8"–1/2", then trimmed into 2-1/2" x 5-3/4" rectangles. You may gently whittle and sand the bark for a rounded look if you wish. Drill two 3/16" holes in each slat, about 3/4" from each short edge.

Step Two Weave a 6" dia. wreath and a 7" dia. wreath out of grapevine. The larger wreath surrounds the bottom rim of the bucket, while the smaller wreath fits inside the top rim. Using thin vine or twine, attach each slat to the plywood circle through their matching holes and around the larger wreath, wrapping your way around the rim. Lash the tops of the slats to the smaller wreath in a similar way. Cut the door hole between two slats with a coping saw, then tack a strip across the threshold cut from pine scrap.

Step Three With a sharp knife or hatchet, split the 18" twig into quarters 7-1/2" into one end. Fan these out into rafters and wire them securely to the bucket rim. Each rafter should extend 1" over the rim. Wire the remaining grapevine to the rafter ends to form eaves, then continue spiralling it up to form a conical frame, wiring it to the rafters as you go.

Step Four The bundle of straw surrounds the post, then fans out over the roof frame. Hold it in place with rubber bands around the post, then tie and wrap with thin vine or twine from the top down. Tie it down through to the frame as you spiral out over the straw, then around the eaves. Clip off the rubber bands. Trim the excess straw around the eaves with heavy scissors. A top loop can be woven as a wreath through a hole drilled through the post top for hanging.

Mosaic Twig Treehouse

This woodsy cottage belongs up in the trees amidst breezy boughs. It can be sized to suit many species of birds, and decorated with whatever patterns your twigs inspire.

Materials List

2 *1 x 10" x 15" Wood planks*
   1 x 10" x 10" Wood plank
2 *1 x 8-1/2" x 10" Wood planks*
2 *3/8" x 9" x 13" Plywood*
   Assorted twigs
28 *1" dia. x 9" Bamboo*
2 *Tin cans*
   10'–16' Multi-pronged trunk post
   Glue and assorted nails

Step One The chamber can be constructed out of most any 3/4" stock, preferably rough-sawn for a rustic look. Cut the roof peak out of both 10" x 15" planks at once leaving 10" corner edges. Cut an entry hole in one of these.

Step Two Glue and nail the 8-1/2" x 10" side planks to these to form the walls, lapping the larger planks over the smaller ones. Let dry, then glue and nail the 10" x 10" base plank to the bottom edges.

Step Three The shape of the twigs you find may help determine the patterns you add to the walls. The distinctively curved corner braces used on the front of this house are two halves of the same twig, carefully sawed in half. The fence pattern and door frame are split twigs cut and bent to fit, then tacked into place. Pre-drilling the nail holes will prevent splitting the twigs. A Y-shaped twig is glued into a hole drilled below the door for the perch.

Step Four The remaining walls can be decorated with twig mosaics. You may want to sketch a pattern on the wall before tacking the larger split twigs on to outline a particular shape, such as a star. Smaller twigs, perhaps of contrasting color, can then be cut to fit inside and around the outline and tacked into place.

Step Five If you plan to permanently attach your house to a post, install a lag screw through the floor and into the post before affixing the roof. If your post is multi-pronged, top nail the other flush-cut branches through the floor as well.

Step Six Cut 9" lengths of bamboo between the knuckles and split them in half. Pre-drill and nail a row of upturned halves on each plywood roof panel. Then pre-drill and nail rows of downturned halves over these, lapped like a tile roof.

Step Seven Pre-drill and nail the roof panels on top of the chamber. Open and flatten two tin cans. Bend them lengthwise to conform to the roof ridge, then pre-drill and nail them in place.

Thunderbird Tipi

Who's to say that certain native species wouldn't want to emulate the habitats of their human counterparts. A child could have lots of fun making and decorating this piece, then waiting to see who sets up camp.

Materials List

      1 x 9-3/4" dia. Pine base
7 *1/4" x 15"–16" Dowels*
      1/4" x 6" Dowel
      1/4" x 2-1/8" Dowel
      1/4" x 1-3/4" Dowel
      11-1/2" x 23" Canvas
      String
      Painter's caulk
      Glue

Step One After cutting the circular pine base, drill seven 1/4" holes about 5/8" from the edge. They should be somewhat evenly spaced, about 1/2" deep, and angled slightly toward the center. They can be widened as necessary to accommodate the tipi poles.

Step Two Make diagonal cuts on one end of each of the seven poles, plus the 6" dowel. This creates a more natural effect. You may even prefer to use straight branches instead of storebought dowels.

Step Three Glue three of the poles into somewhat evenly spaced holes, and tie them together with string about 4" from the top, before the glue dries. Glue in and tie the remaining four poles in the same manner, then the 6" dowel that supports the top flap. Squirt glue all around the top lashing to secure the juncture. Let dry.

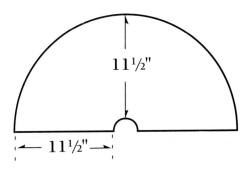

Step Four Cut a semicircle from the canvas as shown in the diagram. Save the scrap. Try wrapping the canvas around the poles, check for fit, and trim as necessary. There should be ample canvas touching the base to glue a seam.

Step Five Run a bead of glue around the base where the canvas skirt will rest. Run beads of glue down the outside of each pole and around the top lashing. Lay the canvas gently around the frame, and gently press it down over all the glue seam. Run a wide bead of glue inside the overlapping edge, then press it gently closed. Let dry.

Step Six Opposite the vertical seam, cut a 1-1/4" x 1-3/4" oval door, 2" from the bottom. Cut a 3" x 4" triangular flap from the scrap canvas, then glue it over the 6" dowel and onto the tipi wall. Cut a 1" x 2-1/2" panel of scrap canvas, then glue it as a V-shaped awning over the door hole. Let dry.

Step Seven Indent one end of the 2-1/8" dowel with a round file. Glue and nail the 1-3/4" dowel to this end to form the perch. Drill a 1/4" hole in front of the door, and glue it in place.

Step Eight Caulk the entire apex of the tipi, including the flap, as well as the door awning, vertical seam and base seam. Let dry. Prime and paint the entire piece with exterior grade paint. Designs can be painted on with hobby enamels. A feathered spear and other toy accessories can be added.

Bat House

Bats aren't birds, but mammals that can devour 500 insects per minute! They're harmless to humans, yet becoming endangered. A house this size can sleep a colony of up to 30 bats. This is a fun project for kids to help with.

Materials List

2   *1 x 12 x 15" Pine*
2   *1 x 12 x 9" Pine*
    1 x 10-1/2" x 15" Pine
2   *1 x 12 x 13-7/8" Pine*
    1 x 4 x 34" Pine
    1/2" x 14" x 25" Plywood
    Glue and assorted nails
    2-1/2" Bolt and nut

Step One You may want to use cedar for the box (painted blue in the photo) instead of pine, for better weather resistance. First cut 3/4" dado grooves lengthwise into the 12 x 9" side panels. There should be two 3/16" deep grooves on 3" centers to channel the inner partitions. Next, cut 3/16" deep grooves about 1" apart, lengthwise across one of the 12 x 15" panels (not shown in photo). Do this again with both 12 x 13-7/8" partition panels.

Step Two Glue and nail the 12 x 15" panels to the 12 x 9" sides, butting the corners, with all grooves facing inward. Glue and nail the 10-1/2" x 15" roof snugly on top. All seams should be tight to prevent leaks. Let dry.

Step Three Cut a 21" length of 1 x 4 for the tree mount. You may wish to jigsaw a bat head outline at one end and tail at the other, as in the photo. Bevel cut the remaining 13" of 1 x 4 as a mounting shim. Glue and nail the shim to the center of the tree mount, bevels up. Glue and nail the box to the center of the shim. This double seam can be reinforced with a 2-1/2" bolt through all three boards up toward the lid (not shown in photo).

Step Four Paint both partitions and the box interior flat black. Glue and nail the partitions into the dadoed grooves. They will be flush with the bottom of the box (unlike the photo, which has an angled roof).

Step Five Cut a bat silhouette from 1/2" plywood. Paint it well to seal the laminations. Paint the entire structure as you wish, then glue and nail the bat emblem proudly on the house.

Bats in the Belfry

Here's an elegant way to control your insect population, even if your neighbors think you're a little batty. Try mounting this in a shady spot near a garden.

Materials List

4	*1 x 11-1/4" x 24" Pine*
2	*1 x 10-1/2" x 14-1/2" Pine*
	1 x 10-1/2" x 10-1/2" Pine
4	*13-1/2" Triangles of 1/4" plywood*
	54" of 1-1/2" Decorative molding
	Floor flange
	1/2" x 3/4" x 10-1/2" Pine
	Bell
	Lathe-turned spire
	Glue and assorted finishing nails

Step One Each of the wall panels could be solid 1 x 12, two planks of 1 x 8, or 3/4" plywood. The overall dimensions can also be varied, along with corresponding adjustments for interior panels. After cutting the four wall panels, use a jigsaw to cut the window openings. The flat bottom sill should be 8" below the top edge. Mark the semi-circular arc with a compass. These windows measure 6" x 6", and should be 3/8" off-center.

Step Two Cut the two interior panels of solid 1 x or 3/4" plywood to fit snugly inside whatever sized chamber you're building. These can be inserted and nailed into place as simple butt joints or into dado cut grooves. Since these panels will partition the three sleeping compartments, be sure to rip cut horizontal grooves on both sides to facilitate the bat's foothold. Grooves that are about 1/8" deep and wide should be spaced 1–2" apart, and should be cut on the facing interior walls also.

Step Three Cut the square panel that forms the roof of the compartment to fit, either butted or dadoed into place. A standard 1" floor flange can be screwed onto the center of this panel. This will accommodate a 1" steel pipe, threaded at the top end, which can be used as the mounting post. The method used here utilized a 1-1/4" dowel post which is inserted into a 1-1/4" hole cut halfway into the roof panel. It is stabilized by a 3-1/4" square block with a 1-1/4" hole. The block slips down the dowel and is glued into place, flush with the bottom edge of the interior panels, into which it snugly fits. Use a hole saw to cut the holes.

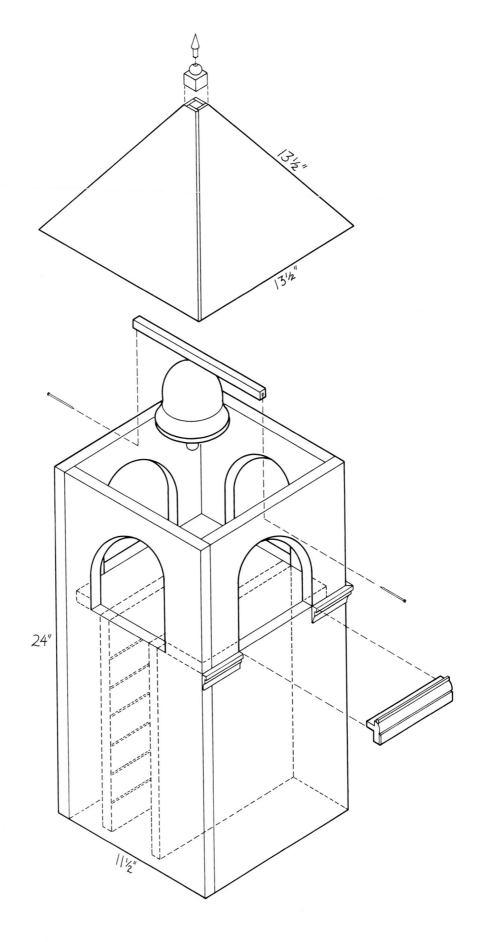

13½"

13½"

24"

11½"

Step Four Join the wall panels one corner at a time with glue and nails. Before attaching the last wall panel, insert the roof panel and secure it with glue and nails. Join the last wall, let dry, then sand all corner seams.

Step Five Insert the two interior panels, and secure them with glue and nails. Rip cut the 1/2" x 3/4" pine bell support, then cut a length to fit the top inside of the belfry. Find an old bell, or turn one from wood on a lathe like this one. Attach it to the support, then install the assembly with glue and nails.

Step Six Measure and cut the decorative molding to form the four cornices. It is wise to cut the miters first, hold them in place to mark the window edges, then make the straight cuts. Glue and nail them into place along a pre-marked horizontal line. The four sill moldings can be cut from the same molding and turned upside down, or from different molding. Cut and install these in the same manner.

Step Seven Cut the four 13-1/2" equilateral triangles that form the roof from 1/4" plywood. The edges that will join can either be miter cut or bevel cut for butt joints. If you choose to insert a block (as shown in the photo), bevel cut the top corners to fit. Otherwise, you can simply drill a hole in the finished roof to accept a dowel spire. To join the roof, run a bead of glue or silicone sealant on one upper edge of each panel, then lean them together and let dry. The seams can be reinforced by lightly tapping small brads into the joints, or gluing dowels or beveled strips into the inside seams.

Step Eight The spire can be lathe-turned, composed of doll house fittings, carved, or a sharpened dowel with beads threaded over it. Whatever its size and shape, it will be glued and nailed into a corresponding hole at the apex of the roof. This roof has a faux copper finish, but the color scheme is up to you. The finished roof assembly is glued and nailed atop the belfry. The top wall edges can be beveled for a stronger glue seam if you wish.

Honeymoon Hideaway

The urge to hole up in this birdie bunga-low will prove irresistible to the nesting instincts of all true love birds. And you won't mind cleaning up after each mating season using the handy pull-out drawer.

Materials List

2   *1 x 5-1/2" x 9" Pine*
    1 x 7-1/2" x 8" Pine
    1 x 6-3/4" x 8" Pine
    1 x 3-7/8" x 5-1/2" Pine

2   *1/2" x 7-5/8" x 12-3/4" Plywood*
    1/4" x 4" x 6" Plywood

3   *1/4" x 2-3/8" x 5-1/8" Plywood*
    1/4" x 2-1/2" x 3-1/2" Plywood

2   *5-7/8" 1/4-Round molding*
    1/4" Lath scrap
    1/4" x 3" Dowel

2   *Eyescrews*
    Glue and assorted nails

Step One Cut tapered bevels on both long edges of the 3-7/8" x 5-1/2" base block at 80°. Cut an 80° bevel on one short edge of each of the 5-1/2" x 9" side panels. Cut a tapered bevel at 60° on the opposite short sides.

Step Two Mark and cut the elongated pentagons from 1/2" plywood, following the diagram. In one pentagon, cut a 1-5/8" hole upper center with a hole saw. Then cut the bottom third off, 4" from the bottom, for the drawer panel.

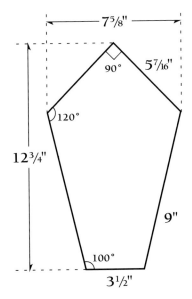

Step Three Glue and nail the whole pentagon to the base and sides, then join the upper pentagon section to this assembly. Glue and nail the 8" pine roof panels with a butt joint, then glue and nail the roof to the top of the chamber.

Step Four Cut 80° tapered bevels on both long edges of one 2-3/8" x 5-1/8" plywood panel (drawer bottom). Cut an 80° bevel on one long edge of the other two panels (drawer sides). Taper cut the 2-1/2" x 3-1/2" plywood (drawer back) so that the bottom edge measures 2-5/16". Glue these panels to the lower pentagon face, forming the drawer. Reinforce with brads after the glue is dry.

Step Five Cut the 1/4" lath scrap into 1/2" widths for fence and shutter slats. The same can be used for cross pieces. Cut picket points on the fencing, and attach as you wish. The windows can be painted on. Cut more scrap for the cross piece under the front gable after mitering and attaching the 1/4-round. The signs are also cut from lath scrap, glued and tacked into place.

Step Six Cut a crescent moon from the 4" x 6" plywood, paint it white, then glue and tack it to the back gable. Install the two eyescrews on the roof ridge, unless you prefer to post mount this house. Drill a 1/4" hole 1" below the entry hole. Cut a 2-1/4" length of dowel and glue it into place.

Step Seven The remaining 3/4" dowel is used to attach the miniature birdhouse, which is an optional feature. It is cut from 1/16" stock and glued on. The entry hole is drilled into the block, with a nail for the perch.

New England Town Hall

Here's a taste of colonial Americana at its finest. This architectural relic of early democracy could host a variety of species—even partitioned as a house for martins. And as with the old town meetings, you are free to interpret the consensus of this design.

Materials List

	1 x 12 x 22" Pine base
	1 x 12 x 20" Pine ceiling panel
2	*1 x 12 x 16" Pine walls*
2	*1 x 12 x 9-3/4" Pine walls*
	1 x 8" x 8" Pine
2	*1/2" x 9-3/4" x 20-1/4" Plywood roofing*
5	*1-1/4" x 11-1/4" Dowels*
	1/4" Plywood or solid stock
	1/8" Solid stock scrap
	2-1/2" x 2-1/2" x 10" Pine
	1-5/8" x 1-5/8" x 6-1/2" Pine
4	*1/2" Wooden beads*
	Roof shingles
	Bell

Step One First, cut the base, the four walls and ceiling panel from 1 x pine. The ceiling panel should be cut with a 45° bevel on both long sides to fit the roof panels. Use a jigsaw to cut all the door and window openings in the wall panels. If you choose to make this a martin house, construct inner partitions from 1/4" plywood to create between 8–12 cubicles in a bi-level configuration. Cut your doors and windows accordingly. Refer to the chart on pages 14 and 15 to accommodate other species.

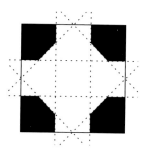

Otherwise, wall up all the openings except one front door with scraps of 1/4" plywood. Then glue and nail this structure together as shown in the exploded view drawing. Let dry.

Step Two Cut the 1 x 8" x 8" pine panel diagonally into two right triangles. Then cut both roof panels from 1/2" plywood. The top ridge seam can be miter cut or lapped with a butt joint. The eaves can be cut with a 45° bevel so as not to detract from the bottom tier of shingles. Glue and nail this roof assembly into place, starting with the triangles. Let dry.

Step Three Cut eight 1-1/2" squares from the 1/4" plywood or solid stock. Bevel cut the top edges, then use a hole saw to cut 1-1/4" holes through their centers. Insert the four 1-1/4" dowels into these blocks, and glue them into place to form the front portico.

Step Four To accommodate the spire, cut two grooves across the roof ridge, toward the front, 2-1/2" apart and to a depth of about 1". Using a coping saw, cut out a 2-1/2" square through the roof panels. Make this opening as snug a fit as possible for the 2-1/2" square spire base.

Step Five The spire is the crowning glory, whether you copy this one or free-form your own. This 2-1/2" square base rests on the ceiling panel. The belfry is opened up at the top by making a series of 3" cuts down from the top, then chiseling out the center (see illustration). Cut and chisel the straight angles before the diagonals.

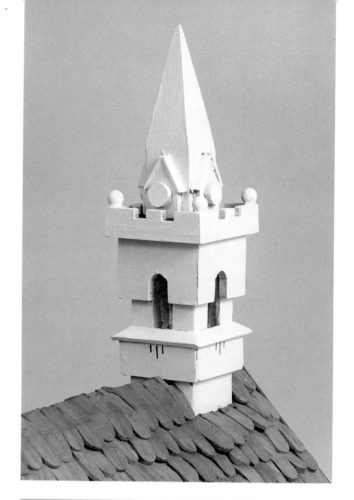

A mitered 1" skirt of 1/4" stock is added just beneath this opening, and capped with beveled and mitered strips of 1/4" stock. Decorative cuts may be added before assembly. The mitered upper fascia is cut from 2" strips of 1/4" stock, including arches cut with a coping saw.

The 1-5/8" square upper spire is bevel cut to a point. Arched panels of 1/4" stock are glued and nailed around the bottom edge, then framed by long rectangular strips of 1/8" stock. 5/8" circles of 1/8" or 1/4" stock can be applied to these. Use a 1-1/4" eyescrew with glue to secure this upper assembly to the center of the 3-7/8" square of 1/4" stock that forms the ceiling plate. A small bell is attached to the eyescrew. Glue and nail all this to the four prongs of the spire base. Mitered 5/8" strips of 1/4" stock form the notched rails. Wooden beads adorn the corners, attached with glue. Dowels can also be used to secure the balls into the rail corners.

This entire structure is firmly secured into the roof assembly with glue. The roof/spire seam should be caulked with waterproof sealant.

Step Six All the remaining trim on doors, windows, roof gables, etc. is cut from 1/4" stock to fit, then glued and nailed into place with small brads.

Step Seven Cut four 3/4" mitered strips of 1/4" stock to form the front and rear roof edge caps, then glue and nail into place. The shingles can either be purchased ready-made as doll house trim, or cut from solid 1/8" stock. Apply successive beads of silicone across both roof panels, and apply each tier of shingles from the bottom up. Every other row is staggered and filled with half shingles on each end. You can paint the structure traditional white or as you wish to enhance the trim.

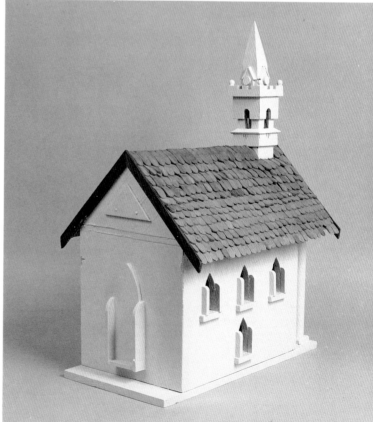

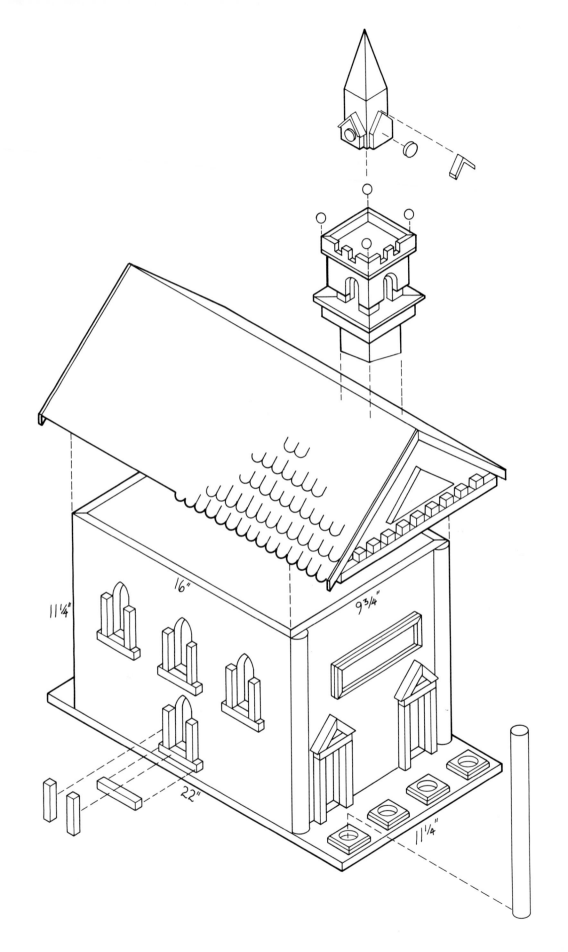

16"

11¼"

9¾"

22"

11¼"

Credits

Projects designed and constructed by:

Ron Anderson
(pages 74, 94, 108)
Don Daniels
(pages 56, 112, 121)
Mark Dockery
(pages 53, 70, 79, 96, 100, 128, 132, 136)
Mike Durkin
(pages 78, 80, 82, 84, 86, 98, 102, 105)
Harold Hall
(pages 119, 120)
Bobby Hansson
(pages 50–52, 126)
Michael Hester
(page 72)
Claudia & Bob Osby
(pages 53, 88, 92, 114, 116, 130)
Ralph Schmitt
(pages 59, 62, 64)
Fox Watson
(pages 67, 138)

Project design assistance by:

Thom Boswell
(pages 72, 74, 79, 82, 86, 88, 92, 98, 102, 114, 116, 130, 132, 136)

Gallery displays courtesy of:

Blue Spiral I, Asheville, NC
(pages 30, 31, 33, 36, 38, 44, 48)

Photography location courtesy of:

The Wright Inn, Asheville, NC
(pages 103, 139, 142)

Bird feed consultant:

Sally L. Coburn

Artist's Directory

Ron Anderson
115 Sue Ann Court
Sterling, VA 22170

Don Bundrick
P.O. Box 84
Tallulah Falls, GA 30573

Carol Costenbader
34 Deerhaven Lane
Asheville, NC 28803

Don Daniels
P.O. Box 939
Locust Grove, OK 74352

Mark Dockery
8 Busbee View Road
Asheville, NC 28803

Mike Durkin
c/o I. Ellis Johnson School
815 McGirts Bridge Rd.
Laurinburg, NC 28352

Marshall Fall
Rt. 1, Box 291-B
Hendersonville, NC 28792

Debra Fritts
385 Waverly Hall Circle
Roswell, GA 30075

Harold Hall
1203 Lake Martin Drive
Kent, OH 44240

Bobby Hansson
P.O. Box 1100
Rising Sun, MD 21911

Michael Hester
244-B Swannanoa River Rd.
Asheville, NC 28805

Mana D. C. Hewitt
947 Laurie Lane
Columbia, SC 29205

Bryant Holsenbeck
2007 Pershing Street
Durham, NC 27705

Barry Leader
122 West High Street
Elizabethtown, PA 17022

Bruce Malicoat
129 E. Vates Street
Frankenmuth, MI 48734

Claudia & Bob Osby
P.O. Box 976
Brevard, NC 28712

Charles Ratliff
183 New Avenue
Athens, GA 30601

David Renfroe
407 Big Pine Road
Marshall, NC 28753

Ralph Schmitt
75 Broadway
Asheville, NC 28801

Randy Sewell
38 Muscogee Avenue
Atlanta, GA 30305

Susan Starr
1580 Jones Road
Roswell, GA 30075

Paul Sumner
5721 N. Church Street
Greensboro, NC 27405

Fox Watson
50 Greene Drive
Black Mountain, NC 28711

West Olive Folk Art
8370 160th Avenue
West Olive, MI 49460

Index